TUNISIA TRANSITION INITIATIVE (TTI)

FINAL REPORT

Program Title:	**Tunisia Transition Initiative (TTI)**
Sponsoring USAID Office:	**USAID/OTI Washington**
Contract Number:	**DOT-I-00-08-00035-00/AID-OAA-TO-11-00032**
Contractor:	**DAI**
Date of Publication:	**July 2014**
Author:	**DAI**

CONTENTS

ABBREVIATIONS

AQIM	Al Qaeda in the Islamic Maghreb
AST	Ansar al-Sharia
BTD	Bridge To Democracy
COP	Chief of Party
CR	Country Representative
CSO	Civil Society Organization
CVE	Countering Violent Extremism
DAI	Development Alternatives, Inc.
DCR	Deputy Country Representative
DDGS	Direct Distribution of Goods and Services
FOG	Fixed Obligation Grant
GM	Grants Manager
GOT	Government of Tunisia
GOTV	Get Out the Vote
IED	Improvised Explosive Device
IK	In-Kind Grant Agreement
ISIE	Instance Superieure Independente Electorale
LGSA	Limited Scope Grant Agreement
M&E	Monitoring & Evaluation
NCA	National Constituent Assembly
OTI	Office of Transition Initiatives
PDO	Program Development Officer
PLO	Procurement and Logistics Officer
PO	Purchase Order
QRF	Quick Response Framework
RCD	Rassemblement Constitutionnel Democratique
RSO	Regional Security Officer
SG	Standard Grant
SRS	Strategy Review Session

SST	Senior Strategy Team
STTA	Short Term Technical Assistance
TTI	Tunisia Transition Initiative
UGTT	Union Generale Tunisienne du Travail
USAID	United States Agency for International Development
UTICA	Union of Industry, Commerce, and Handicrafts
YEDA	Youth Empowerment and Development Association

EXECUTIVE SUMMARY
PROGRAM DESCRIPTION

On January 14, 2011, long-time President Zine el-Abidine Ben Ali fled Tunisia after one month of youth-led protests fueled by socio-economic grievances, corruption, and political repression. The Revolution ushered in a wave of political excitement for Tunisia and prompted the initial steps towards democracy and political reform. Tunisia held historic elections on October 23, 2011, drawing 58% of eligible voters to the polls to vote for representatives for the National Constituent Assembly (NCA). Ennahda, a moderate Islamist party, won 40% of the seats – more than any other political party but not an outright majority. As a result, Ennahda formed a coalition with two secular parties: Ettakatol and Congress for the Republic. The NCA's mandate was to draft Tunisia's new constitution.

USAID's Office of Transition Initiatives (OTI) sought to support Tunisians in their pursuit of a democratic society and more equitable, responsive, and legitimate governance. In particular, the program, known locally as the Bridge To Democracy (BTD), provided material and technical support to communities, civil society organizations (CSO), and local institutions to help build democratic resiliency, increase citizen participation in democratic life, and bolster positive change. USAID/OTI's program objective was to create viable space for the transition to succeed by implementing high impact and high visibility programming to improve citizen-government dialogue on transition issues. To achieve these objectives, the Tunisia Transition Initiative (TTI) program worked with a variety of local partners, including Tunisian individuals, organizations and government representatives to identify and implement key programmatic initiatives that were catalytic in nature, with activities primarily focused on two complementary program areas: encouraging new and emerging civil society groups to contribute to the national dialogue; and promoting civic engagement through small community development projects.

TTI's programmatic response to the country's transitional context was through the implementation of activities designed to strengthen mutual trust between citizens and their government in the transition process, encouraging constructive dialogues and supporting different stakeholders in advocating for sustainable solutions to the country's challenges. In accordance with OTI's programming approach, TTI's activity strategy was designed to be flexible and responsive to changing conditions and needs, laying the foundation for sustainable solutions. As part of its overarching strategy, TTI supported activities that allowed Tunisian citizens from marginalized regions to participate in the political reform process and the formation of new political institutions.

Activities were generally small, short-term and in-kind, and were intended to be relevant to the concurrent political context. TTI focused on providing tangible benefits at the community level in the short term to create the space required for true democratic change to take hold, thereby supporting dialogue around national level issues central to the transition. The program focused on political and geographical "tipping point areas," being people and issues central to making the Tunisian transition to democracy a success in the central interior governorates of Kasserine, Gafsa and Sidi Bouzid through their Sbeitla Regional Office, as well as the Greater Tunis area through its headquarters office.

PROGRAM OBJECTIVES

With the overall program goal of creating space for the transition to succeed, TTI upon implementation identified eight sub-objectives which would guide programming in order to achieve improved democratic engagement between Tunisian citizens and their government, being the following:

- Activism: To promote citizen activism

- Civic Engagement: To increase citizen participation in political processes

- Civil Society Organizations: To increase CSO leadership capacity

- Social Media and Media: To increase social media/media's capacity to report objectively

- Information: To increase citizens' access to and demand for information

- Marginalized Groups: To increase the voice of marginalized groups in the political process

- Countering Violent Extremism (CVE): To strengthen the sense of belonging to moderate Tunisian society for at-risk youth

- Tolerance: To increase the acceptance of the diversity of views

These eight objectives were further refined in October 2013 into four streamlined objectives which guided activity development for the final 8 months of the program: CSOs, Civic Engagement, Marginalized Groups and Countering Violent Extremism.

RESULTS

TTI activities strengthened the efforts of CSOs, associations and other groups to organize platforms through which citizens conveyed their priorities to local government and national reform entities, and took part in discussions about the formation of a Constituent Assembly, drafting of the new constitution, and creation of new representative government institutions. TTI assistance helped established and emerging groups to communicate their ideas, propose solutions and engage with decision makers to move from confrontational protest to generation of constructive projects. Its work with municipalities and CSOs improved their working dynamic and built trust among the citizenry, such as through the maintenance and rehabilitation of living spaces and community centers. TTI also supported small scale local level economic and social projects that complemented national dialogue activities by targeting citizens whose sense of economic marginalization might challenge the political transition. Small scale activities helped defuse opposition to the political process by connecting local economic development to national decision-making. Communities drove selection of activities and participated in project implementation, ensuring greater buy in and more organic programming support.

By leveraging a variety of media and communications advocacy efforts, the project promoted tolerance, respect for diverse views and backgrounds, decreased social and political tensions and positively addressed political violence to allow citizens to both air grievances and work collaboratively with the government to address concerns. It also prioritized youth initiatives and issues through activities such as training workshops, debates, web activism, artistic expression promotion and town hall meetings to acknowledge their seminal role in driving political activism and thereby alleviate frustration over lingering political and economic issues in constructive ways. TTI promoted the role of women and women's rights in Tunisian democratic society by partnering with female journalists, CSO leaders and the Ministry of Women's Affairs to design programming that encouraged equal opportunity for all and raised awareness of the importance of women's inclusion in the public and community space.

Over the course of its program, TTI funded 272 grant under contract, short term technical assistance and direct distribution of goods and services activities valued at $12,429,697 to over 180 partner organizations.

COUNTRY CONTEXT

TIMELINE

December 2010 – Protests break out over unemployment and political restrictions, quickly spreading nationwide

January 2011 – President Zine al-Abidine Ben Ali goes into exile amid continuing protests; Prime Minister Mohammed Ghannouchi announces an interim national unity government

March 2011 – Date for constitutional assembly election announced for 24 July 2011

June 2011 – Ben Ali is tried in absentia for theft and sentenced to 35 years in prison

October 2011 – Parliamentary elections are held, with Ennahda Islamist party winning the largest share, though short of an outright majority

November 2011 – National Constituent Assembly meets for first time

December 2011 – The NCA elect Moncef Marzouki as President and Hamadi Jebali as Prime Minister

May 2012 – Hundreds of Salafist extremists clash with security forces and attack a police station in Jendouba in a dispute over Salafist attacks on alcohol venders

June 2012 – Ben Ali is sentenced to life in prison over the killing of protesters during the 2011 Revolution

August 2012 – Thousands protest in Tunis against moves by Ennahda to reduce women's rights

February 2013 – Opposition leader Chokri Belaid is assassinated, prompting violent protests; Jebali resigns after his ruling Ennahda parts rejects his proposals to form a government of technocrats, prompting former Minister of the Interior and Ennahda spokesperson Ali Laarayedh's appointment to Prime Minister

May 2013 – Violence erupt in the Tunis suburb of Ettadhamen and Kairouan due to clashes between police and Salafist Islamists from Ansar al-Sharia

July 2013 – Opposition politician Mohamed Brahmi is assassinated, prompting further mass demonstrations, a general strike and poplar calls for the government to resign

October 2013 – Governing Ennahda party agrees to hand over power to a caretaker technocrat government of independent figures tasked with organizing new elections in 2014

December 2013 – Ennahda and the mostly secular opposition agree on the appointment of Mehdi Jomaa, former Minister of Industry, as interim Prime Minister

January 2014 – Jomaa officially sworn in as Prime Minister; a 146 article draft constitution is completed and adopted by the NCA with 200 in favor, 12 against and 4 abstaining

February 2014 – US Secretary of State John Kerry visits Tunisia to demonstrate support for the country's transition and discuss security assistance, as well as invite Jomaa to DC to speak to President Obama

April 2014 – Jomaa travels to the US to speak with President Obama and discuss the US's continued commitment to advancing democracy in Tunisia and other ways support can be given for the transition

May 2014 – Tunisian Assembly approves electoral law, allowing officials to set dates for legislative and presidential polls

June 2014 – Voter registration begins on June 23

2011 ELECTIONS AND AFTERMATH

The National Constituent Assembly elections were conducted on October 23, 2011. More than 5,140 Tunisian observers and 530 international observers were mobilized. The turnout was 77.65% among the 4.1 million who registered voluntarily and 14.2% for the rest of the voters. The electorate was estimated at 7.2 million. The Tunisian Islamist party, Ennahda, which was harshly repressed under the old regime but legalized after the Revolution, secured 41.7% of votes, obtaining 89 seats of the 217 seats at large; other parties included the Congress for the Republic, Ettakatol, and Social Democratic Party.

Following the successful conclusion of the elections, a report by the National Commission of Investigation of Corruption and Embezzlement of the former regime was presented on November 11, 2011. The 345-page report shed light on the extent of corruption by the former regime involving ministries, banks, customs, media, the justice system and the commercial sector. It denounced abuses on a large scale, expropriations, blackmail, insider trading and criminal practices, revealing the involvement of persons other than simply the extended clan of the presidential couple. Furthermore, the creation of an independent National Coordinating Structure for Transitional Justice was announced officially on November 15, 2011. The aim of this body was to establish transitional justice mechanisms to judge those responsible for corruption and crimes under the former government and compensate victims accordingly.

On November 22, the Constituent Assembly formally began its work and elected as its Speaker the Ettakatol party leader, Mustapha Ben Jaafar, after which the constituent assembly voted on November 23 on the composition of two NCA commission bureau members: the commission tasked with devising the internal rules and the Commission tasked with preparing the final text of the public authorities' provisional organization. Tunisia adopted on December 1 a short interim constitution that enabled the designation of the president and of the head of government (Prime Minister) who would lead the country until the adoption of a final constitution followed by general elections.

The provisional government outlined a program of economic and social development initiatives based on the implementation of comprehensive reforms to address the strategic aspirations of the Revolution. This program, which grew partly out of various initiatives of the previous Government, aimed to strengthen competitiveness and create sustainable national growth and improve standards of living based on greater social cohesion. Meanwhile, the Government also emphasized that the establishment of this new domestic economic policy should be accompanied by continued efforts to integrate into the global and regional economies, particularly vis-à-vis Europe and the Arab Maghreb Union.

RISE OF VIOLENT EXTREMISM, POLITICAL INSTABILITY AND ECONOMIC CRISES

Despite these early signs of progress, the beginning of the drafting process of the Constitution was troubled from the start with infighting between the Assembly members; debate on Article I and the role of Sharia law in the Tunisian legal system took over a month. This period was also marked by a growing crisis of confidence between citizens and officers of the three political parties forming the ruling coalition. Bloc resignations were common and there was widespread public dissatisfaction. Offices of political parties including Ennahda became the target of attacks from protesting citizens.

Uncertainty in many aspects of life in Tunisia continued to characterize the transition period. In addition to political and social uncertainty, the central west of the country experienced frequent electricity failures and drinking water shortages, even though rainfall reached record levels in

2012. Frequent sit-ins were held in public areas and on main roads, general strikes paralyzed some communities, and Salafist influence spread considerably, with some media reporting that Salafists controlled more than 400 mosques throughout the country.

Furthermore, the macroeconomic consequences of the Revolution were severe in the short-term. In addition to material damage (estimated at 4% of the country's GDP), the Tunisian economy faced increased insecurity and social tensions, as well as a collapse in tourism revenues (-46%) and a sharp decline in foreign investment (-17.8%). There was a sharp rise in commodity prices, additionally, and the ability of the financial system to attract external funding for projects and Tunisian companies was strongly affected by the increase of the country's risk.

The Libyan crisis had a major impact on Tunisia in terms of lost remittances and the return to unemployment of thousands of Tunisians who had been employed there. Labor unions continued to demand a larger and larger slice of a shrinking pie. Geopolitical uncertainties in the region negatively influenced the economic recovery, and gave rise to widespread disillusionment with the failure at that point of the Revolution to provide tangible dividends to the population.

On the security front, President Marzouki extended the state of emergency nationwide in response to the perceived increased threat of criminal and political violence. The September 14, 2012 attack on the US Embassy and the American Cooperative School of Tunis resulted in the deaths of five demonstrators and injury to 105 others, including 65 security forces, as well as severe damage to both facilities. In response to the situation, the State Department ordered the departure non-essential staff and family members from Tunisia, and published warnings for U.S. citizens considering travel to the country.

The government appeared unable to respond effectively to the deepening crises and lost more and more credibility with its citizens. In a Sigma Consulting poll published on September 27, 2012, 70% of Tunisians believed the country was headed in the wrong direction; 86% were dissatisfied with the government's performance on pricing (that is to say, cost of living); 96% believed that the government had failed in the fight against unemployment; while 46% were dissatisfied with the performance of the National Constituent Assembly. However, 50% believed that the government had made progress on press freedom, with 58.8% were satisfied with the security. Only 60% of respondents were confident in the country's future, against 80% and 90% at the beginning of the Revolution.

Meanwhile, in the absence of border controls, politically motivated violence worsened. Clashes between security forces and terrorist groups rocked the country during the month of December, believed to have been carried out by a branch of Al Qaeda in the Maghreb (AQIM). There were discoveries of weapons caches in the interior and parts of Tunis, worsening the perception of insecurity throughout the country. Members of the Ennahda-affiliated League of the Protection of the Revolution carried out attacks on demonstrations of the country's major labor union, UGTT, and attacked the events of other political parties, particularly Nida Tounes.

In early 2013 violent extremist groups of unconfirmed origins or affiliations were believed to have established a presence in camps in the western part of the country, specifically in the regions of Kef and Kasserine's Mount Chaambi. The camp located in Mount Chaambi near Kasserine was surrounded by improvised explosive devices (IEDs) that killed two soldiers and wounded several others, and there were perceptions that a section of the Salafist movement may have armed jihadists linked to AQIM.

The violence reached crisis point when key opposition leader Chokri Belaid, a Tunisian lawyer and opposition leader with the Democratic Patriot's Movement party, was assassinated in front of his home in February 2013. Many Tunisians believed that Ennahda or its supporters were behind the assassination. The murder came as a profound shock in Tunisia, which has a long history of political repression, but where targeted political violence is virtually unheard of. This event triggered widespread unrest and a general strike calling for the entire cabinet to step down. In May 2013, the government denied the Salafist jihadist organization Ansar al-Sharia (AST) permission to hold its annual congress in Kairouan. As a result, clashes erupted in Kairouan and Ettadhamen between supporters of AST protesting the ban and police action, causing many injuries among law enforcement and locals as well as the death of one citizen. In the late summer and fall there was continued violent confrontation between western extremists and Tunisian security forces, most notably the brutal killing of eight soldiers on July 29 near Mount Chaambi, as well as four separate IEDs found in Tunis and Mount Chaambi, resulting in two deaths.

STAGNATION OF POLITICAL PROCESSES AND PROTESTS

The political crisis deepened on July 25, 2013 when Mohamed Brahmi, an NCA member and founder of the People's Movement party from Sidi Bouzid, was also assassinated. Together with Belaid's assassination, the country plunged into deepening political crisis, giving rise to months of sit-ins and protests calling for the dismissal of the government on one hand, and loyalty to the sitting party on the other. This physical manifestation of the political opposition resulted in increasing polarization along conservative and moderate party lines, making it more difficult to develop programming activities that avoided unwittingly getting caught up in the debate. For example, even engaging Tunisians in an activity around the Constitution could have been construed as expressing an opinion about the progress of the process, especially in relation to the most contentious articles. Contemporary USAID experiences in other countries had shown that even the perception that the Embassy or US Government was taking a position could have disastrous consequences.

This also provoked a mobilization of Tunisian society amongst different groups of protesters demanding the departure of the Ennahda-led government and the selection of a date for elections. Shortly after, in response, Ennahda loyalists staged counter demonstrations. There was an extended showdown in Bardo, in the center of Tunis, where the two sides were kept apart by Tunisian police and razor wire. Many NCA members from the opposition suspended their membership in protest. This physical manifestation of the political opposition nonetheless resulted in increasing polarization, which quickly became overtly partisan along conservative and moderate party lines. UGTT and the Union of Industry, Commerce, and Handicrafts (UTICA) made repeated efforts to resolve the gridlock with the major political parties, but the initial refusal of the current governing body to resign resulted in a stalemate for many weeks. Talks began between the political parties and labor unions under the premise of partially replacing the current governing with a group of technocrats to organize transparent elections, while the NCA would remain intact to finish its mandate of creating a constitution for the country and creating an electoral body but this yielded no results for an extended period, worsening anxiety and dissatisfaction over the stagnating political process.

Political divisions persisted not only in opposition ranks but also within Ennahda's ruling coalition. Of particular concern was the lack of progress on finalization and public consideration of the Constitution, a critical step (along with election of a new Instance Superieure Independente Electorale – ISIE – and ratification of an electoral law) before new elections could be held. The role of civil society organizations and a free press were still not clearly established and the long standing grievances that triggered the revolt against Ben Ali – unemployment, corruption, and inequality – were likewise perceived to have been ignored. Other key Constitutional issues continued to be the proper role of religion in the affairs of the state, women's rights, and personal freedoms. This was a major obstacle to the holding of elections on schedule, as voter enrollment would need to be underway by mid 2013 in order to hold valid, transparent elections before the end of 2013 as promised.

The NCA established a Constitutional Drafting and Coordination Committee tasked with coordinating commission work, preparing a general report on the constitutional drafting project before its submission to the plenary assembly, and establishing a final version of the report. All these rules were supposed to ensure a transparent and accessible constitutional drafting process, but in practice the public, civil society and media were not always aware of what was occurring at each stage and could not access information easily, with most of the debates taking place behind closed doors. Commission reports were not posted on the NCA website, impeding meaningful citizen involvement.

NATIONAL DIALOGUE AND THE CONSTITUTION

On October 5, 2013, twenty-one political parties signed a roadmap document which outlined four major steps in the political process: forming the ISIE; finalizing the Constitution; designating a transitional technocrat government; and finalizing the electoral code (including setting an elections date). The original plan for the National Dialogue was that it would begin with the resignation of the sitting government in favor of a pre-election technocrat caretaker government. The national dialogue began at the Ministry of Transitional Justice and Human Rights under the sponsorship of the Quartet, composed of the UGTT, UTICA, the Tunisian Union of Human Rights and the Union of Lawyers.

The process stumbled again on November 6 when political parties were unable to agree on a new Head of Government candidate. In response to the ongoing negotiations by the 21 participating parties regarding the choice for the new head of government, Houcine Abbassi, Secretary General of the UGTT and leader of the Quartet made this observation: "They all want candidates customized according to their own interests, when we could simply opt for a standard size, suitable for all." According to Secretary Abbassi, the key to a successful outcome was for individuals and parties to set aside personal agendas and work for the greater good of Tunisia: "It is not very difficult to succeed. It is sufficient that each of the parties concerned renounces his ego, supporters and interests. The solution will be found."

Secretary Abbassi cited three main requirements for a potential candidate: competence, independence and integrity. He revealed that there was a sense of compromise among the political parties and confirmed that no single political party controls the national dialogue. The Quartet extended the original deadlines more than once hoping to reach a consensus, noting with caution, "There are parties who wished to benefit from a new deadline, requesting additional 7 to 10 days. We accepted their request and gave them an appointment with us next Saturday, December 14. "

On December 14, Mehdi Jomaa, the former Minister of Industry, was chosen as the head of government; of the 19 parties present, only 11 voted. On December 17, Mouldi Jendoubi, Deputy Secretary General of the UGTT, announced that the Quartet gave the roadmap to Jomaa, leading to the first demonstrable signs of progress in months. On December 30 heated debate took place in the National Assembly related to the passing of the Finance Act and the 2014 budget, particularly the Karama budget which was a compensation budget for people that suffered during the dictatorship.

On January 8 the National Constituent Assembly elected a president and nine members of the Independent High Authority for the Elections. Elected by a vote of 153 out of 208 votes cast, Chafik Sarsar became the new president of ISIE. On January 9, the head of government Laarayedh submitted his resignation and that of his Government to the President of the Republic, in accordance with the requirements of national roadmap, and interim Prime Minister Jomaa was officially sworn in as the official head of government in the position of Prime Minister on January 29.

Following these confirmations, on January 14 during the brief plenary session, members debated items 103-108 in the chapter of the judiciary, helping to reconfirm a more positive trend towards progress. As a result, Tunisia's new constitution was adopted on January 26, 2014 by the National Constituent Assembly, and was published on February 10 in the Official Journal of the Tunisian Republic; with this publication, the Constitution became the law of the Tunisia. Several international organizations subsequently called for a review of existing Tunisian legislation so all laws would conform to the Constitution.

PREPARING FOR PARLIAMENTARY ELECTIONS

In a statement released March 6, 2014, the President of the Republic announced the cancellation of the state of emergency in Tunisia, which was an encouraging sign of a return to normalcy.

The debate on the electoral law began on the afternoon of April 14. Ennahda emphasized the importance of preserving national unity and consensus, as the debate has focused on the issue of exclusion. Of particular note, some deputies expressed their refusal to support a law excluding former members of the old regime under the Democratic Constitutional Rally (RCD), while the Wafa movement launched a campaign for an article preventing ex RCDistes to be present in the next election. A further dividing point among deputies concerned the disenfranchisement of the military and security forces, as well as the use of "guardianship" (i.e. assistance) for illiterate voters, which some deputies saw as a violation of the principle of "secret suffrage" for citizens. Finally, the issue of campaign financing continued to be debated.

Examination of sections of the electoral law continued slowly in the National Constituent Assembly. Chapters on general provisions and voter requirements did not provoke significant disagreements and delays, mainly due to the absence of members, which made it more difficult to achieve the necessary quorum when votes were called. More significant debate, however, centered on the chapter related to eligibility for election. The first section of the chapter (Article 18) proved controversial due to an amendment proposed by members of Ennahda, CPR and Wafa to modify the article of exclusion by replacing "incapacity under this Act" by "incapacity provided by law in general." The amendment, though ultimately rejected, received 93 favorable votes (109 were required).

These debates were finalized in April 2014 ahead of their self-imposed April 27 deadline and Tunisia's interim parliament on May 1 approved a new electoral law to govern legislative and presidential polls, due to be held by the end of 2014. Three years after the country's Revolution and three months after the approval of a new constitution that was hailed by Western countries as a transition towards democracy in the birthplace of the Arab Spring, the law was passed by 132 votes in favor, 11 against and nine abstentions in the 217-member National Constituent Assembly.

The planned elections aim to create permanent institutions in the country, however the body responsible for organizing the elections, the ISIE, faced constraints with regards to budget, office headquarters and initial lack of legislation on which to base its work. Moreover, the ISIE has said that it would need between six and eight months to organize elections once the law was passed. Its head, Chafik Sarsar stated he was "absolutely" convinced that elections could now go ahead as planned before the end of the year.

The legislative polls are to be held on a single, first-past-the-post basis by constituencies, rather than fixing a threshold, while the presidential election is to be staged over two rounds and will require a majority vote. Sarsar said the vote's transparency would be guaranteed by the new electoral law and by more than 1,000 international observers who had been invited to monitor the ballot. On May 21, the ISIE announced that voter registration would begin on June 23.

On June 18, the General Legislation Commission of the NCA adopted the elections calendar proposed by the ISIE, and on June 23 official voter registration began. The legislation elections were set for October 26, 2014 and the presidential elections were set for November 23, 2014.

STRATEGY REVIEW

PHASE ONE: INITIAL SET UP AND ELECTIONS

TTI began its initial programming phase in May 2011 by identifying issues within the project's scope and manageable interests, particularly with an eye towards supporting the country's National Constituent Assembly elections in October of that year and the constitutional process writ large. To establish the project's primary foci of governance, tolerance, communication and transparency, the Chief of Party and Country Representative and Deputy Country Representative sought to identify the key program challenges and issues for the first six months in order to select the right priorities given the project's limited funding and achieve the most impact in the project's initial two years. The team also sought to ensure that all team members were included in the program's design, especially given the distance between its offices and activities so as to leverage local knowledge and resources. Also present in their minds was the acknowledgement that many Tunisians were suspicious about working with the US Government, and so careful consideration about combatting anti-American sentiment was key.

Importantly, elections activities were designed to promote information dissemination and transparent communications about the voting process, civic responsibilities, the role of civil society and the media, and promotion of democratic values while recognizing that security could be a major destabilizer in this process. As such, the project sought to complete activities that promoted these nationally important concerns by targeting youth, the media and CSOs, with a particular focus on the governorates of Tunis, Ariana, Manouba and Ben Arous in the Greater Tunis area, as they

A voter education on wheels center

encompassed a critical mass (forty percent) of the population and were broadly representative of the wider issues present throughout the country. Furthermore, while the Revolution started in the interior, the protests, strikes and demonstrations with the most visibility during the Revolution took place in Greater Tunis, bringing together and building connections between many different people from different areas throughout the country. Furthermore, key partners such as national ministries, the national media, NCA members, and well established associations were predominantly controlled from Tunis, and as such that area had the greatest capacity for nationwide influence.

The next strategy decision was identifying those specific partners whose involvement would generate the most catalytic impact. With the easing of political restrictions and incorporation constraints, Tunisia experienced a dramatic increase in the number of CSOs as well as newly motivated local government officials, however given the years of repressive governance, their respective capacities and leadership abilities varied greatly. The key was to ascertain who were the revolutionaries, who were the change agents, who had the strongest interest in the transition, and whom was the project trying to influence, inspire and engage. In order to identify the right partners, the project also sought to establish the key beneficiaries, chiefly those who in one way or another were disaffected and disconnected from the transition. The project sought to prioritize programming that targeted urban and disillusioned youth, particularly young unemployed men who had the greatest possibility to revert violence or disruption. Additionally, activities were untaken which engaged government officials with unrealized impact or potential whose passive involvement in the transition negated their ability to inspire meaningful, progressive change. Lastly, the national media lacked direction, organic support and the journalist skills or knowledge to adequately inform the populace objectively about the decisions being made and the responsibilities they held to impact those decisions as part of a participatory democracy; TTI designed activities to counteract this.

PHASE TWO: EXPANDING THE DEMOCRATIC SPACE

Following the successful completion of elections, and especially after the first Program Performance Review in June 2012, TTI moved from a nation-wide implementation strategy to a more targeted approach in seven select governorates, being Kasserine, Sidi Bouzid, Gafsa and El Kef through its Sbeitla Regional Office, and Tunis, Ariana, Ben Arous and Manouba in the Tunis Headquarters Office, while continuing select nationwide programs focusing mainly on tolerance promotion and use of public media. These governorates were selected through the project's utilization-focused approach to Monitoring and Evaluation (M&E). This approach dictated that the M&E components were designed to be used by and be relevant to programming. Data gathered was used to refine program design based on findings and lessons learned, being therefore a collaborative effort allowing the learning processes to inform and improve the program, specifically through the sub-strategy process.

To execute activities, TTI selected CSOs and other partners to implement grants which aligned with the project's strategy, using a collaborative approach with partners to design and implement

A "Constitution Tent" in Tunis distributing blank copies of the constitution to encourage Tunisians to contribute to the drafting process

the activities. Furthermore, its work under Phase One helped the project to better identify strong local partners for its activities' implementation, including NGOs, INGOs, government officials, companies, civil society organizations, and groups of individuals which the team had identified as change agents, such as progressive community leaders from across the political spectrum, social entrepreneurs, artists or musicians, youth or women focused activists, and social media based CSOs. By partnering with these key groups, the project was better positioned to target individuals and groups who could positively impact the transition, including CSOs, media, artisans, government officials, community leaders, marginalized groups, etc. These groups were typically either already actively engaged in their communities and political processes, or they were the "fence-sitters" and undecided; TTI determined that both groups had the capacity to participate in and contribute to the democratic transition.

Programming was targeted to do more activities in selected "tipping point" areas, focusing on achieving a depth rather than breadth of comprehension and ownership of key initiatives that provided an opportunity for local problem solving and advocacy. TTI utilized mapping data to better target their activities and achieve maximum impact, such as on grants which disseminated a slogan on the referendum, shared information about the constitutional drafting process, educated voters about elections procedures and key issues, or helped to clean up neighborhoods so that youth had a safe place to congregate after school. By working with well-connected, influential groups and organizations, the project supported activities and ideas that were easily disseminated and adopted beyond the immediate scope of individual grants, using various elements of the media as a means to further build momentum and engage Tunisians from all political, social and economic strata. Activities also recognized the importance of balancing messaging or training campaigns with the tangible delivery of goods or services to more visibly demonstrate signs of positive change.

PHASE THREE:

For Phase Three, TTI used the confirmation of the extension year as awarded in December 2012, the February 2013 Strategy Review Session (SRS), and a change in project leadership to systematically review the technical approach and ensure that activities maximized impact for the resources expended. One of the key outcomes of the SRS was a reaffirmation of the need to more fully involve Tunisian staff in the development and operationalization of the program strategy, thereby better fostering a sense of ownership and capitalizing on local staff's knowledge, experience and networks. As a result, the Country Representative (CR) and Chief of Party (COP) created the Senior Strategy Team (SST), composed of the Head of Field Office, Senior Program Development Manager, Regional Program Manager, and M&E Manager. The SST solicited program-wide input into defining program success and breaking out the program objectives of "creating space" and "fostering dialogue" into actionable, measurable impacts that allowed program staff to better plan and target activities against clearly articulated goals. This created a framework for eight sub-objectives.

If Tunisian citizens, CSOs, media, and government officials advocate, engage, have increased capacity, report objectively, use information, lead, accept diversity, and have a sense of belonging, TTI argued then that democratic space for the transition to succeed could be created, allowing citizens to pursue a democratic society. To support the creation of this space, TTI designed activities during Phase Three around eight sub-objectives: activism, citizen engagement, CSO capacity, media and social media, information, marginalized groups, tolerance, and countering violent extremism (moderation). Six sub-objectives primarily supported the participation of citizens, media, government, and civil society in political processes, such as elections, constitution, and local governance; two sub-objectives primarily fostered the development of democratic ideals and culture among citizens:

- **Activism** – Citizens were frustrated with the slow pace of change and evolution of political processes they had experienced immediately following the Revolution, most notably the election and constitutional processes. Community leaders and activists lacked the skills, networks, knowledge, and opportunities to advocate for change and accountability in a democratic manner. By promoting citizen activism, TTI encouraged a broad range of Tunisians to participate in their country's transition in new and previously under-utilized methods within civil society.

- **Civic Engagement** – Though many Tunisians understood democracy in a theoretical sense, few understood how it was practiced. Citizens lacked knowledge on general democratic principles, responsibilities of citizenship, and the means to actively and meaningfully participate, especially with the constitution and local governance structures. TTI sought to increase citizen participation in these political processes.

- **CSO Capacity** – CSOs multiplied rapidly after the fall of the regime due to liberalization of political and social organization outside of the auspices of the government. These nascent CSOs lacked the management and leadership skills, extensive networks, and democratic knowledge to support and lead civic engagement and activism; in response TTI created activities designed to increase CSOs' leadership capacity.

- **Social Media/Media** – Media and social media played an important role in the Revolution, and continued to do so in Tunisia during the Constitutional drafting process. 50% of young Tunisians used Facebook as their primary news source around the time of the Revolution. The prolific yet nascent social media and traditional media structures suffered from a lack of knowledge, skills, and experience to report objectively, which led to the spread of misinformation and rumors. Citizens, journalists, and bloggers lacked a clear understanding of media's role in a democracy, which TTI activities sought to address in order to increase social media/media's capacity to report objectively.

- **Information** – There was no tradition of open and transparent communication in the government and there remained little dissemination of reliable information on political processes (in particular the elections and Constitution) and general governance under the NCA. This caused frustration, spread of rumors and misinformation, suspicion, and lack of clarity about the true state of the political process. In addition, information based decision making was not well established on the part of the NCA. Citizens lacked information about the political processes and key democratic principles that are necessary to make decisions and participate in a democracy. This objective addressed the need to increase citizens' access to and demand for information.

- **Marginalized Groups** – Women and youth played an important role in the Revolution; however had been largely apathetic or unengaged since the Revolution. Women and youth lacked the leadership skills, networks, and access to information necessary to have a voice in the transition and participate actively in political processes. This objective sought to increase the voice of marginalized groups, particularly women and youth, in the political process.

- **Tolerance** – Post-Revolution, Tunisia struggled with its national identity and became increasingly polarized. Individuals across the spectrum tried to narrowly dictate what defined a Tunisian, despite a rich history of diversity. In some cases, frustrations with differences of opinions resulted in political violence. Citizens lacked the understanding of the role diversity plays in a democracy and the skills to be able to debate and discuss topics among individuals with different backgrounds and points of view. This objective underscored activities whose goal was to increase the acceptance of a diversity of views as a democratic value.

- **Countering Violent Extremism** – The perception of an increasing extremist threat increased in the aftermath of the Revolution; evidence suggests that young Tunisian men were becoming a recruiting base for jihadists in Syria, as they remained disconnected from the political process. TTI developed the CVE objective to design activities which strengthened the sense of belonging to moderate Tunisian society for at-risk youth.

Within the framework of these eight sub-objectives, activities were designed to be short, responsive to the current political context, flexible, and directly supportive of the program goals. Activities typically lasted one to five months and funding was usually in-kind. Activities were prioritized based on the following factors: fit within the sub-strategy, including targeted sub-objectives and beneficiaries; link to prior and future programming; potential to inspire civic action; comparative advantage of TTI intervention; funding availability and prioritization; capacity to support implementation; and degree of innovation.

As a result of this participant driven approach, TTI programming became more responsive and better focused on impact. As discussed above, the SST led the entire team in the development of a revised strategy aiming to create space to allow Tunisians to participate in the democratic transition. Development teams devised governorate sub-strategies to tailor these principles to local conditions. Concurrently, the design of individual activities placed a renewed emphasis on the selection and design of activities that went beyond raising awareness to catalyzing citizen action in the democratic space. Activities were likely to encourage follow on actions by participants, beneficiaries and their communities, or build upon previous successful activities in some way.

During this time, the SST also developed a Quick Response Framework (QRF) to better position the team to respond to the fast changing political and security context, programming

A Quick Response activity in Siliana, encouraging citizens to "Be a Piece of the Solution"

contingencies that demanded an immediate programming response. TTI developed a range of programming options that could swiftly be adapted to the situation in order to effect immediate impact in the aftermath of such an event, such as the sudden outbreak of political violence (including high profile assassinations, violent protests, high profile terrorist attacks on Tunisian civilians or security forces) or dramatic political shifts (such as actual or de facto abandonment of democratic transition, a successful power grab by unelected or peripheral players, unilateral dissolution of a currently established legislative or judicial body). Objectives for the QRF included the dissemination of counter narratives, making available actionable information, encouragement of peaceful discourse and action, offering democratic institutions or officials the opportunity to engage with youth, giving members of the public the opportunity to air grievances or concerns, and undermining extremists' desire to exploit uncertainty, fear or a political or security vacuum. In order to do so, activities would be designed to reach target communities through online or mass media forums, facilitating organizations and CSOs' leadership strengthening and therefore presenting a united front on a given issue, enabling engagement between the public and elected officials as appropriate, and soliciting immediate programming ideas from TTI staff and trusted partners.

The rollout of the revised program strategy with streamlined activity clusters were important adaptations to the changing political context and the identification of countering violent extremism as an increased program priority. This was immediately put to the test as the Tunisian political situation became increasingly unstable beginning in February 2013 with the assassination of Chokri Belaid, further complicating programming in some respects. His death was followed by a second high-profile assassination of opposition figure Mohamed Brahmi in July. TTI's immediate response to these developments was the rollout of quick response activities in Tunis and the interior, which included high profile tolerance messaging and a series of community fora in the interior that coincided with the traditional breaking of the Ramadan fast held throughout the country.

In response to political violence in the summer of 2013, TTI programming staff sought ways to foster open dialogue about the transition through various activities that allowed participants to select the agenda and drive the conversation, perhaps in response to an artistic performance rather than an overtly political event. TTI also renewed its emphasis on encouraging pluralism and open conversation through the program strategy's tolerance sub-objective, spreading a message behind which all sides of the political divide could unify. Following the recommendations of the August 2013 PPR and during the October 2013 SRS, the SST streamlined the eight sub-objectives to four: CSO capacity, civic engagement, marginalized groups, and countering violent extremism. These four sub-objectives guided the programming through its final months, including the roll out of a CVE pilot program beginning that fall, a renewed emphasis on educating the citizenry on the constitution, and preparing for elections.

The injection of CVE funds earlier in the year had come at a timely point in Tunisia's transition, in that extremism (as manifested in the two political assassinations, violent clashes between Tunisian security forces, and the declared intent of extremist groups to derail the nascent democratic process) had become a much more prominent feature of the political landscape. In response to team input and a comprehensive review of drivers of extremism in Tunisia, TTI targeted CVE programming around the following two drivers of violent extremism in Tunisia: perceptions of social exclusion and marginality and social networks and group dynamics (identity and sense of belonging).

These inclusion focused activities coincided with a series of activities aimed at educating the citizenry as a whole regarding the importance of the constitution, its contents and their impact on the daily lives of all Tunisians. With its ratification, furthermore, the Constitution paved the way for TTI to begin to address the issue of preparing the country to register and vote in legislative and executive elections to be scheduled towards the end of 2014, and remained an important milestone in the transition that the program sought to support in spite of the fact that the elections would be held after the project's close. The team initially intended to deliver voter education grants ahead of the elections, but because of Sbeitla's shorter closedown schedule, the team proposed to develop and implement nation-wide voter education for all grants out of the Tunis office. However, by early February it became apparent that the process of finalizing the electoral law would be lengthier than anticipated, and there would not be enough hard information about the process available in time to devise the materials and roll out voter education or training of trainers before program close. TTI scaled back its plans to roll out a suite of direct voter education grants, instead implementing a number of successful individual activities around the theme of elections in the project's final months.

PROGRAM HIGHLIGHTS, ACHIEVEMENTS, MAJOR ACTIVITIES

TTI aimed to foster Tunisian ownership of emerging political processes and build the foundation for civic engagement in democratic life. Over three years, TTI worked with local partners to support national-level democratic processes, as well as community priorities to demonstrate tangible dividends of the Revolution. Activities responded to emerging political issues and focused on increasing civic engagement, building capacity of civil society organizations, inclusion of marginalized groups in political processes, fostering tolerance, and countering violent extremism. This was achieved through a variety of programming approaches and methodologies, encompassing a variety of target audiences and implementation areas, all designed to achieve maximum impact and resiliency to facilitate a successful transition to fully inclusive democratic governance and society.

CIVIL SOCIETY ORGANIZATIONS

CSO IMPACTS

One of the key components of this democratic reform transition is the establishment of a functional civil society that helps engage the citizenry in a robust public dialogue about issues that affect them. During the 23 year reign of Ben Ali, CSOs had almost no space in which to operate. The regime made registration nearly impossible for most associations in Tunisia, and

when organizations were permitted to operate, they had to accept the intrusive involvement of a ruling family member as a pre-condition of registration. Since 2011, thousands of organizations were created, nearly all of which are relatively inexperienced and lacking in the expertise necessary to take a leadership role. Throughout its three years of implementation, TTI supported activities that allowed Tunisian citizens from various backgrounds to participate in the political reform process and development of new political institutions. TTI activities supported the efforts of CSOs, associations and other non-government groups to organize platforms through which citizens conveyed their priorities to local government and national reform entities, and took part in discussions about the formation of a Constituent Assembly, drafting of a new Constitution, and creation of new representative government institutions. In particular, the program provided material and technical support to communities, civil society organizations, and local institutions to help build democratic resiliency, increase citizen participation in democratic life, and bolster positive change. To achieve these objectives, the TTI program carefully selected its partners to help identify and implement key programmatic initiatives that were catalytic in nature and which strengthened mutual trust and dialogue between citizens and their government to achieve sustainable solutions to the country's challenges.

By utilizing art sport and music initiatives for social programs; incorporating new technologies and media; and clustering and sequencing activities which built on one another over time to create networks and resiliency within the developing space, TTI CSO programming helped established and emerging groups to communicate their ideas, propose solutions and engage with decision makers to move from confrontational protest to constructive and cooperative reform.

The very first activity launched out of the Sbeitla office worked with the Network of Associations for Citizenship and Development of Kasserine to develop an assembly initiative to allow 60 key civic-action groups from throughout the governorate to hold the first meeting of its kind were civil society organizations and average citizens participated in an open dialogue on subjects related to democratic transition and organization. In the governorate, dynamic and energized citizens, led by young university graduates in particular, had been building a brand-new civil society, creating a multitude of private self-help organizations focusing on raising consciousness about Tunisia's new democracy and helping to create job opportunities, however as the number of such organizations grew, a core group of leaders began to worry that they were becoming too diffuse and ultimately too weak to advance their goals and speak with one voice to power. This activity convened the founding assembly in order to agree on objectives and strategy for their activities, selecting a steering committee and vote on the statute they were required to submit to the authorities to receive official recognition, thereby granting greater legitimacy to their organizations and by working as a coalition enhance the effectiveness of their participation.

In order to consolidate their impacts and ensure that the many disparate groups joined together to provide a substantive voice of citizens' needs to the government, both groups recognized that designated public spaces where members could come together outside their homes to work and collaborate was the next step in the development of the civil society space. TTI in response to a request from a group of CSOs and the leaders of Medenine, Kasserine, and Mahdia provided workshops in each area between the local government and the CSO community to designate and furnish a public CSO House, provide training on how best to facilitate its usages and coordinating a charter to best manage the space and set the foundation for future collaboration and a vibrant civil society. Discussions were then held between the hundreds of activists and government officials participating on the creation of an effective partnership which allowed those engaged to draft and sign a charter between these associations to form a single body, capable of bringing together diverse actionable objectives and serving as the interlocutor for local government officers and institutions to engage and effectively lobby for their needs.

Supporting situations which encouraged positive interactions between citizens and government

officials was part of a strong effort TTI made to foster a spirit of unity among all stakeholders. This included training civil society organizations in networking and monitoring development projects on a local level. In partnership with the Global Development for Siliana, a consortium of local associations, TTI organized a two-day interactive forum and series of workshops intended to examine the state of development in the governorate. The activities brought together organization leaders, activists, and government representatives with the goal of creating a common platform for communication regarding development problems in Siliana. The forum was successful in generating three commitments on behalf of stakeholders: the creation of a civil society network in Siliana; the creation of a committee representing the civil society network to work with the government in tracking local development projects; and finally, planning for further training sessions for local associations.

It was also important to ensure that these organized CSOs continued to reach out and recruit the involvement of youth actors so that they remained relevant and inclusive. Since the youth-led Revolution, universities had been at the forefront of political discourse and civic action. Beyond the halls of academia, universities often afforded youth their first opportunities to explore and experiment with local politics and civil society through introduction to extracurricular clubs and activities. During the former regime, youth activism on campus was heavily monitored by the Ministry of the Interior and was limited to one or two clubs that were tied to the former regime's political party.

Since the Revolution, many youth had indicated interest civic engagement but did not have the information about how to start clubs or register with existing clubs, especially in the interior of Tunisia where there were fewer well organized university clubs. A youth and political participation study commissioned by TTI in the summer of 2013 indicated that a majority of youth were not involved in associations and were unaware of existing organizations and initiatives. TTI then designed an activity to provide information to students in Gafsa about how to join university clubs and CSOs in order to increase citizen activism. Through an in-kind grant with Sawty Gafsa Association, this activity supported the organization of an Open House Day on the university campus of Gafsa which supported approximately 19,000 students. There was advertising and registration for clubs within the university, and university clubs and local CSOs were invited to exhibit their achievements and activities with small booths. Additionally members Association Internationale des etudiants en sciences economiques et commerciales/ International association for students in economics and commercial sciences, a well-organized university youth association, was invited to give a presentation for the public on how to start a club and the necessary administrative steps to register a club in a university setting.

As part of its capstone series of activities, TTI produced both an Artivist Workshop and CSO Fair as opportunities to bring together all the program's partners from the life of the project to showcase their strengths, abilities and increased capacities, as well as provide an additional opportunity to network and exchange information. For its Level Up Artivist Workshop, TTI increased the capacity and knowledge of Tunisian CSOs in communications, sustainability and programmatic impact, especially in the political process and in preparation for the upcoming Tunisian elections, in order to increase CSO leadership capacity. The activity produced a four day cutting edge workshop and speaker program for approximately 70 Tunisian youth led and youth focused CSOs which focused on the key elements necessary to effectively plan and sustain their own activities while collaborating with others engaged in influencing the Tunisian political process. The activity underscored that CSOs themselves must continuously grow and adapt to the changing social, technological, and artistic context in order to stay relevant and effective, and that one way of doing this was to build on the expertise of activists in other countries who had supported or participated in other political transitions. The workshops brought together 25 internationally renowned experts to lead sessions which balanced the fundamentals of building CSO capacity and improving their effectiveness with cutting edge sessions led by acknowledged world experts in campaigning, cybersecurity, web design and game and app creation for change, sustainability, advocacy, whistleblowing, privacy and political activist platforms. The agenda was split into 4 labs (Investigative and Citizens Lab, Legal and Advocacy Lab, Creative Lab and Security Tech Lab), during each of which the moderators were invited to share their experiences on the topic through discussing their connections with the Tunisian context, and culminated in a brainstorming session for the follow on Next Level Up CSO Fair.

On April 18 and 19, the CSO fair and festival known as *Joussour* ("Bridges") was held at The Medina Hotel and Conference Center in Hammamet, weaving together workshops, debates, an expo and cultural performances with messages about the importance of CSOs in the political process, and their value to the Tunisian citizenry. With a combination of workshops, performances, panel discussions, debates and a center for exposition booths, *Joussour* created a festive fair atmosphere intended to increase the interest in and visibility of Tunisian CSOs, as well as to improve the effectiveness and leadership capacity of these CSOs. The exposition hall featured 76 association booths manned by 354 TTI partners where leaders and members could display their accomplishments and promote their work. On-going entertainment both inside and outside the exposition hall was featured with a total of 13 rap, hip-hop, graffiti, music, and other street art performances from TTI partners over both days. Invited guests from international and local NGOs strolled among the booths and engaged in informal discussions with presenters and performers.

A partner's booth at the CSO Fair "Joussour," TTI's capstone event

Additionally, six workshops (on topics ranging from communication to sustainability to programmatic impact) and four panel discussions were facilitated by a team of national and international experts in the fields of activism and advocacy, leveraging their respective expertise to allow the attendees to learn, share and develop specific plans for strengthening the networks and range of tools available for Tunisian civil society to increase its influence in the transition space. Panels on fundraising, sustainable development, effective coalition building and best practices for government collaboration sought to increase the capacity and knowledge of Tunisian CSOs in communications, sustainability and programmatic impact, especially in the political process with an eye towards the upcoming Tunisian elections.

In concert with these activities, Joussour moderated a series of debates on the following four topics: the legal framework of the law organizing the work of associations in Tunisia; youth as actors of change; success stories from the Lebanon and Senegal; and the role of the civil society to sensitize citizen about the importance of voting.

On the second day, 163 youth from target TTI communities, as well as members of the public, attended the event, thereby increasing the exposure and messaging beyond the immediate participants. There were 13 smaller multi-stage musical and dance performances and two large evening performances on Friday and Saturday night, respectively. The *Joussour* program built off of three successful years of TTI partnerships with CSOs in Tunisia, particularly in the Greater Tunis area and the central governorates of Gafsa, Kasserine and Sidi Bouzid, showcasing their achievements, allowing them to make connections with each other and with other donors, and raising public awareness and support of civil society throughout the country.

EXEMPLARY PARTNERS

Young Leaders Entrepreneurs

YLE initially approached TTI looking for ways to contribute in assisting the youth of Tunisia to

take part in youth entrepreneur and leadership training programs. This spawned an activity entitled "New Generation Initiative" which sought to prevent teenagers about to enter university from sinking into oblivion and extremism due to lack of a clear understanding of how verbal violence and lack of civilized attitude may lead to a shattered generation full of resentment and hatred, ultimately resulting in the failure of the Revolution's democratic transition. TTI then partnered with the organization again to

A young Tunisian women participates in the "One Billion Rising for Justice" campaign holding a balloon stating "You Are the Revolution"

sponsor youth based reform brainstorming and initiatives creation in addition to leadership training and project management guidance as part of their "Countdown: Build Tunisia in 20 Hours" activity, as well as a subsequent project in held in concert with the worldwide "One Billion Rising For Justice" campaign that brought mass global action working to end violence against women and promote gender equality. Throughout the project's numerous activities with this awardee, YLE proved an exceptional partner in providing youth mentorship and activism training, creating established networks of youth supporters, successfully utilizing traditional and new media outlets to support their endeavors, and working closely with the program to transform their ideas into concrete projects with impactful results.

Sawty Association (Gafsa and Tunis)

TTI first partnered with the at the time newly formed Sawty Gafsa on the Tunisians Share Beirut activity, organizing a three day event in Beirut that brought together forward thinking activists, social media and IT experts, artists, musicians and other creative thinkers to share ideas on freedom of expression, the arts and the use of technology for activism. Sawty was recognized for their work in youth and civic engagement utilizing new media and the arts; through their partnership with TTI, the organizations continued to develop and grow their capacity significantly, especially in the following three areas: presentation and promotion of the values and functioning models of democratic society; inform the mechanisms and characteristics of the Tunisian political system and its actors; and serve as a platform for exchange between Tunisian youth, the state and civil society. TTI went on to partner with Sawty to sponsor political debates, host CSO open houses, conduct training and voter outreach, organize flash mobs on the constitutional drafting process and the importance of active citizenship, production of viral videos celebrating the anniversary of the Revolution and sparking dialogue with political leaders on outstanding issues, sponsorship at the World Social Forum, hold workshops to strategize on ways to increase youth engagement, and organize online campaigns to increase the voice of marginalized groups in the political process. Through their partnership with TTI, the organization grew in membership and capacity, expanding their network of supporters and areas of expertise to ensure continued success beyond the closure of the project.

Art Solution

The cultural NGO Art Solution sought to provide cultural opportunities for individuals to improve their communities, reduce violence and promote tolerance and positive engagement while fighting prejudice through artistic approaches to traditional activism problems. Its members have been active in the reinvigoration of hip-hop and break dance across the different regions of Tunisia, and promotion of street art and legal graffiti as a form of expression. Art Solution networked and trained artists and break-dancers from all over Tunisia and has organized several street break dance events, eventually preparing the young dancers for the Battle of the Year, a worldwide break-dance competition held in Carthage on the 7th and 8th of July 2012. Art Solution has also worked with TTI in different youth centers, identifying talented youth and empowering them by giving access to different resources, allowing them to  share their experiences through a variety of media and forums and providing them with skills that will equip them for their places in the new Tunisia. First partnering with TTI in an activity which provided graffiti artists, professional break dancers and DJs in celebration of the events of and ideals of the Revolution at six youth centers throughout the Greater Tunis area, Art Solution went on to work with TTI on a variety of activism projects designed to entertain, inform and engage youth through public dance performances, professionally recorded tolerance songs and music videos, street art festivals and Artivist workshops. Their work has gained international attention, being featured in magazines such as Paris Match, cultural organizations like the Goethe Institute, and news outlets like Jeune Afrique, spreading their message of the importance of youth activism and street art as vital tools of political engagement and reform.

Touensa

Touensa is dedicated to active citizenship, transparency in government processes, and promotion of democratic principles, seeking to raise awareness of the importance of democratic participation, voter accountability and political mechanisms. Founded immediately following the Revolution via a citizen pact created on social networks, following the fall of Ben Ali the initiative aims to contribute effectively to building a democratic Tunisia by strengthening nascent civil society and the capacity of average citizens to fight for their priorities. Through this lens, TTI worked with Touensa on a variety of projects, including bus tours of the country featuring outreach teams to educate citizens about the Constituent Assembly elections and the creation of active citizenship television spots featuring the specially designed Lahlouba character to share information about the elections process. Through their work with TTI, Touensa has enabled citizens to be more knowledgeable and empowered to productively engage in their developing democracy, strengthening emerging networks of civil society and better placing them to engage in civic life.

ACT Khamem ou Karrer

TTI first worked exclusively with the Tunisian women's association ACT Khamem ou Karrer to disseminate the popular Lahlouba comic book at the World Social Forum in 2013, having been

exposed to their organization during the 2011 Active Citizen Forum, being a large global community of participants and partners within the Active Citizens program and just one of the various CSO networks including the Tunisian Bus Citoyen with which this organization had significant professional connections. Following their involvement in TTI's Women's Day celebrations in 2012, ACT was engaged in an activity to produce a manifesto and profiles of

Copies of the Lahlouba comic book being distributed at the 2013 World Social Forum.

over seventy Tunisian female activists and role models whose portraits and messages of inspiration were displayed on Tunisia's largest

French and Arabic newspapers in celebration of Women's Day 2013. The activity further established a database of the women's respective associations to help create a platform for women involved in the political process to share their perspectives and experiences with citizens.

Bus Citoyen

Despite the record number of women who participated in demonstrations and rallies throughout the country during the Tunisian Revolution, helping to ensure its success, women were concerned eighteen months later before Women's Day 2012 that their role in the transition was not being recognized nor their voices heard. As such, TTI partnered with Bus Citoyen and numerous other NGO partners to stand together and rally to demand that the government pledge to uphold their rights in the constitution, marching to the Palais Congres with speakers, performers and artistic exhibitions demonstrating their importance in the revolutionary process and their role in a democratic Tunisia. Since that activity, TTI worked with the organization in a number of different capacities to support women's rights, including constitutional information awareness campaigns, roundtable discussions and trainings and tolerance promotion activities designed to build the capacity of Tunisian citizens to engage with their government, and the capacity of CSOs to network together in concert with the government to address the country's outstanding concerns.

Rocking Steps Crew

The Rocking Steps Crew was founded in 2007 by rap musicians, dancers and graffiti artists in Sidi Bouzid who realized that youths who had extracurricular outlets in their lives were better able to resist overtures from extremists. After gleaning break dance moves off the internet as a form of rebellion with their friends, they learned through Facebook of a break dancing competition being held and hitchhiked across the country to get there; they were the last to perform but ended up being first in the tournament. When the Revolution came, they threw themselves into the protests to demonstrate their desire for positive change, but as the transition stalled, they saw more and more young people feeling neglected and alienated turn to violence, drugs and extremism. They decided to create an association to run workshops and events to offer teens an alternative. As part of a street arts festival in Sidi Bouzid commemorating the start of the Tunisian Revolution, TTI first became involved with the Rocking Steps Crew as a grantee working with art students from the local college to paint commemorative murals on public spaces in the city to underscore the importance of artistic freedom of expression and the ways in

which art and culture can be used to convey positive messages about the transition process. Since then Rocking Steps Crew has organized and participated in events and workshops both domestically and abroad in dance, extreme sport, rap, graffiti, DJing, photography, short movies and theater to mobilize youth to express themselves through art and find other like-minded individuals to amplify their voice and contribute positively to the transition process. Their efforts have earned them international acclaim, with coverage being provided by such news outlets as the New York Times, MSN Arabia, Public Radio International and Paris Match.

Mowatinoon Association

Based in the interior region of Gafsa, the Mowatinoon Association is an NGO working extensively on civic education with more than 80 percent of their members being women. TTI worked with the Mowatinoon, meaning "citizen" in Tunisian, initially to support the production and dissemination of thousands of bags with slogans advocating women's engagement and gender equality throughout the governorate during Ramadan in 2012 to further underscore that women's rights are not at odds with traditional cultural values. After the success of this activity, TTI again worked with Mowatinoon to facilitate workshops for women to identify and express the most pressing concerns in their communities to local government officials. The workshops coached the women in ways to better organize themselves, identify actionable concerns, advocate for their priorities and learn how to have meaningful and productive discussion with government officials to effect change. Following the accomplishments of this activity, TTI also worked with the Association to host reconciliation dinners bringing together a cross section of Gafsa's most influential community leaders from civil society, political parties and representatives from influential syndicates for constructive dialogues that foster community cohesion and acceptance of a diversity of opinions.

Fani Raghman Anni

In order to counter the spread of violent extremist ideologies and create a sense of belonging to moderate society, TTI partnered with the famous Fani Ragman Anni youth theater association to produce a series of trainings followed by community theatrical performances on the topics of human rights, tolerance, anti-violence and the role of youth in the transition. Meaning "My Art Despite Myself," the organization brings together youth who write, act, dance and incorporate the visual arts into their performances which usually take place in the streets and often involve specialized movement techniques such as body paint in order to provide direct contact with the public. Their performances with TTI were then filmed and spread online through social media, allowing the youth leaders taking part in these activities to share their experiences and serve as role models for their peers, encouraging them to form their own theatrical clubs and engage positively in their communities.

Munathara Initiative

The NGO group Munathara Initiative was first brought to TTI's attention after their highly regarded televised debate on Al Jazeera Live around the question "Is Tunisia on the Right Path?," where it engaged a thousands of supporters through an online competition, Facebook page, Twitter Feed, mobile app and YouTube channel, which during the height of the project  reached more than three million viewers. TTI then decided to partner with the organization to facilitate a follow up youth debate utilizing their innovative online and outreach methodologies to catalyze participation and interest. Their popularity and expertise were leveraged for the "Tunisian Elections: The Debate Must Start!" grant which began with debate training and culminated in both online and televised youth debates which were then uploaded into social media sites to engage thousands of young people in the political dialogue through mediums they were already literate in, proving such a successful model that it was utilized in other TTI debate activities such as for the university debate series and workshops held in Kasserine, Gafsa and Sidi Bouzid designed to increase youth leadership and confidence, as well as the Women's Day 2014 debate and public speaking skills workshops for activist women in the interior to increase their voice in the political process.

Women & Leadership

The Women & Leadership NGO is committed to raising and reinforcing the socio economic and political role of women in Tunisia, being founded initially to raise awareness of the protection historically afforded to them under the previous regime's Code of Personal Status and other similar laws. The organization is open to all - women and men - and has members from all socio-economic backgrounds and geographic locations, and enjoys a close relationship with Ministry of Women's Affairs and one of the country's largest private micro-finance institutions with a 120,000-strong female client network in more than 60 locations around the country. The well networked and highly motivated Women & Leadership Association first joined forces in a GOTV campaign targeting

women throughout the country to educate them on the importance and value of their participation in the Constituent Assembly elections. The Association's network of women

A poster encouraging Tunisian women to participate in the election

across all of Tunisia helped facilitate rapid, comprehensive campaign targeting women of all ages, backgrounds and means through mainstream and new media forums, which proved especially useful during their panel discussion activity held on the International Day of the Elimination of Violence Against Women. This activity incorporated 250 male and female activists, entrepreneurs, professors, journalists and other opinion shapers to fight for the protection of women's status in Tunisia. Other similar events undertaken in partnership with Women & Leadership include discussions and art exhibitions displaying the contribution of women to the political process, showings of locally produced documentaries about ordinary citizens' experiences following the Revolution, rallies for women's rights, female journalism training, advocacy skills workshops, public debates, constitutional awareness roundtables and student outreach.

YEDA

The Youth Empowerment and Development Association (YEDA) was launched immediately following the beginning of the Tunisian Revolution on January 14, 2011 as a means to reach out to uninformed and disenfranchised youth through NGO-led civic engagement, often incorporating artistic performances and social media to reach out to their communities and

The Fi Houmty Youth Dance Tour organized by YEDA

develop networks of support. YEDA targets primarily youth ages 12 to 26 for training programs and socio-cultural activities that nurture the innovative and creative spirit inherent in the country's young people. It also attracts youth by organizing training programs and discussion circles that bring awareness of social responsibility, developing leadership abilities and cultivating and encouraging the discovery of new talents. They therefore developed a particular interest in the Constituent Assembly elections, seeking to partner with TTI in order to help the youth of the Revolution better participate

in the voting process, organizing activities which trained elections monitors, conducted bus tours throughout the governorates to inform youth about political engagement and interests, reached out to clarify complexities surrounding political parties and the elections, and educated voters about the importance of active citizenry and the democratic process. Subsequent activities grew and evolved from their initial capacity and vision through the assistance of TTI, demonstrating to youth from across the country the importance of art, creativity and freedom of expression in a democratic society through cultural workshops; campaigns to create platforms through which young leaders could develop; dance performances and trainings that advocated for anti-violence; and youth art presentations designed to inspire others to take ownership of their government.

CIVIC ENGAGEMENT AND ACTIVITISM

2011 ELECTIONS

Chief among its first priorities under Phase One, TTI immediately began undertaking activities designed to prepare the country for its first democratic election in decades to be held October

2011 for the National Constituent Authority. The Independent Election Commission, ISIE, began its voter registration process on July 11, 2011, including a campaign encouraging people to register at ISIE facilities, however with only 55% voluntarily registering, the commission automatically registered the rest, precluding these individuals from updating their official residence location or polling station without additional action on their part. While some parts of Tunisia were more marginalized than others vis-à-vis social and economic standards, the entire country was equally in need of voter and civic education given Tunisia's nascent democracy and the evolving political processes, thereby this initial activity reduced confusion on election day, resulting in more citizens actually voting for the Constituent Assembly on October 23, 2011.

Many political parties attempted to manipulate the electorate, and many nascent CSOs lacked the capability to independently educate them accurately, which when combined with the general confusion surrounding the process, presented an opportunity for TTI to produce and distribute materials designed to encourage these marginalized groups to vote and participate in the democratic transition while also conducting anti-corruption campaigns in the face of political manipulation. In order to further encourage individuals to register and vote, particularly marginalized groups such as women, youth and rural dwellers, the program sought to ensure equal male and female participation in the decision making processes, thereby ensuring a transparent and democratic transition. Most of the activity beneficiaries included nascent associations focused on youth whose organizations were led and

Youth participate in a mock election to encourage political engagement

organized by individuals under the age of 25, lending them greater credibility with youth in their respective communities. Grant activities enabled organizations and youth to build new networks throughout the country and conduct different trainings on the electoral process, reminding citizens of the sacrifices made during the Revolution and the importance of their newly re-gained voice. The strategy implemented to meet these objectives was focused on three main points: anchoring democratic values (e.g., awareness, learning and training); monitoring of the electoral process and election observation; and, denunciation of any action taken by any player in the democratic process (e.g., government, political parties, ISIE) that may negatively affect the democratic process. TTI also sponsored NGO-led community level discussions complete with social media tools and hip hop dance performances to draw out youth voters and educate them on the voting process and how to determine one's political orientation. To supplement this, the project educated voters by supporting a group of local NGOs to recruit, train and dispatch education outreach teams, travelling by bus to each governorate of the country to present clear voter and civic education information, as well as the future role of the Constituent Assembly in Tunisia's democratic reform process.

In a short period of time, general voter education activities regarding the democratic process writ large were able to reach beneficiaries across the national landscape in Tunisia. TTI therefore began an activity designing five episodes of an animated television series explaining how Tunisians who did not actively register to vote can indeed still do so, and if they chose also update their polling station within the vicinity of their home of record. TTI also supported the ISIE and 50 NGOs in the production and dissemination of information designed to educate people about the electoral process and encourage citizen participation in the elections. When the day of the elections came, TTI helped to safeguard their transparency through support of ATIDE, an NGO that aimed to be an effective and independent organization representing civil society with local, regional and national institutions and representatives. Together 4,270 elections monitors received voter education training and printed poll watcher guidance manuals before being stationed at a total of 1,300 polling stations throughout Tunisia's 24 governorate, ensuring operations related to voting were consistent with international standards for democratic, honest and free elections, conforming to the guidelines established by the ISIE.

ENGAGING GOVERNMENT OFFICIALS

On the eve of the Jasmine Revolution in Tunisia, the idea of a partnership between civil society leaders and local government officials was unimaginable. However, decades of dictatorial rule left behind a bureaucratic culture unskilled in dealing with a free, democratic and active civil society, while elected officials lacked the experience and skills to effectively communicate with and advocate for their constituents. Furthermore, since the start of the Revolution municipal structures, which had been all but invisible under the previous regime, struggled to restructure themselves due to a lack of resources and lack of capacity, impacting provision of services like sanitation and serving as visible reminders of the long and difficult process ahead. After the successful execution of the Constituent Assembly elections, TTI therefore moved to facilitating greater consultative governance, as the growing divide between citizens and their government threatened to derail the momentum of the transition.

Working with citizen development organizations such as Association Karamaty, Jeunesse Sans Frontieres and Tunisian Association for Political Development, initiatives were launched to bring citizens and their government together around critical areas of daily life, being also key points

for the success of the democratic transition. TTI brought together civil society representatives, NCA members, Governors, local media personalities and youth activists over a series of Iftars celebrating the breaking of the fast during Ramadan. The dinners were well attended by each of the communities and afforded an opportunity for people of various political and ideological leanings to interact with one another in a non-polemical space, meeting their counterparts face to face to discuss the problems that existed in their areas, as well as ways to address them. As a means of stimulating further engagement and discussion, TTI supported a youth led forum as an opportunity for participants to speak their voice about the benefits of local democracy, the importance of local taxation, support for a constitutional referendum and the establishment of an elected regional council chaired by elected representatives, leaving youth more confident that their NCA listened to them and that they could work through established lines of communication to effect positive change. These issues were brought to a national audience when TTI, in partnership with the Association of Tunisian Media and SHEMS FM, produced a town hall radio event to enhance debate and maintain dialogue on key issues, raising awareness about Tunisian political parties and alleviating local frustrations with the transition process.

In order to better inform the agenda of local elected officials in terms of the needs of their constituents, TTI facilitated a dialogue between members of the NCA, local municipal government representatives in Kasserine and social activists to produce the country's first charter for CSO engagement. The initiative was first introduced during a workshop supported to form a network of associations in Kasserine, which also brought to light the lack of public space for CSO meetings and information dissemination. The network lobbied the municipality for support of an incubator for CSOs to work, meet and share information on upcoming projects among themselves and with the government.

Building on the idea that government must be responsive to its constituency, TTI also recognized that the constituency needed to be educated about their role in the transition. Through an In Kind grant to the Center of Strategic Research to Promote Development and Democracy, a two-day workshop led by legislative and governance experts was held in Kasserine on the subject of local governance and the decentralization process of the draft constitution with local CSOs, government officials, political party representatives and activists invited to participate in order to increase citizen participation in political processes and allow relevant stakeholders to ask questions about how the articles will affect them.

NEIGHBORHOOD CLEANUP AND REHABILITATION

Since the Revolution, community structures were weakened and the municipal response to the citizen's needs in terms of cleaning and garbage collection deteriorated for several reasons, including strikes and budgetary mismanagement. One of the most visible issues affecting the country was the large amount of trash that had accumulated since the Revolution, and the Tunisian government did not have the financial or human resources to address the problem. Tunisia used to have a strong Ministry of Environment to clean streets, but since the Revolution this Ministry experienced severe constraints, leading to piles of construction rubble being dumped on roadsides, parklands, soccer fields and forests. Mountains of trash collected on vacant blocks and street corners to be burned every few weeks by local residents who couldn't take the unsightliness anymore and feared the spread of disease, leading to concerns by residents of both health and aesthetics.

The clean-up effort in El Mourouj

The Tunisian government recognized this problem, but without the adequate means to quickly address the problem, launched a nationwide campaign asking everyday citizens to help keep Tunisia clean.The objective behind programming this type of activity was to improve the relationship and build trust between local governance structures and citizens through the maintenance and rehabilitation of living spaces, restoring a sense of normality and trust in the government's ability to provide local services. To achieve this, TTI committed to engaging not only with municipalities but also with civil society organizations in order to mitigate immediate frustrations by providing tangible improvements to local communities.

Exemplary of this type of programming, TTI partnered with the Civic Club of Oued Ellil in Greater Tunis and the Association Karamaty in El Mourouj to bring together the respective communities, local CSOS, and municipal authorities for a two-day event intended to encourage dialogue between community members and government officials. First was held a preparation day with municipality officials and representatives from the community in order to fix the plan of the cleaning campaign and to define what are the key concerns in the community. With this established, the organizers then launched a cleaning campaign of the neighborhoods and their parks through the provision of cleaning materials (wheelbarrows, brooms, garbage bags, gloves, cleaning products) and trash receptacles to be handed over to the municipality at the conclusion of the activity, as well as t-shirts for volunteers working out in the community to further disseminate the campaign's message beyond the media presence in attendance. On the second day, the activity hosted in the cleaned park small activities and workshops for youth including painting and decorating the park wall with graffiti, entertainment and discussions about the situation in Tunisia and how it affects the youth of Oued Ellil, leading to a greater sense of involvement and connectivity within the community with their municipal leaders, as well as decreased frustrations in the face of a concrete and positive manifestation of change.

In the interior, TTI undertook activities in various governorates including Gafsa, where high visibility city beautification initiatives involving dozens of civil society organizations, government entities and volunteers engaged with residents to demonstrate the ability of average

A CVE focused calligraffiti activity in Kasserine that was linked to a clean-up and beautification campaign

citizens to improve their communities together with their representatives. Activities were designed to build mutual trust between local government and community members by supporting a tangible project that directly addressed community needs and engaged citizen support. These projects were also often combined with youth engagement activities such as calligraffiti training or breakdance workshops, where those trained could participate and demonstrate their newly acquired skills publicly, further demonstrating their positive engagement with the community at large. In another activity in Ksar Gafsa, TTI provided supplies and equipment to improve public spaces and support an awareness campaign about the importance of civic engagement, demonstrating the government's commitment to providing for its citizens through new approaches and methodologies. In partnership with a group of parents and teachers from the communities of Lortess and Lela, respectively, TTI cleaned and rehabbed schools to encourage residents to take responsibility for their community and network with government entities, neighborhood committees and CSOs to inform about upcoming activities and coordinate efforts. Finally, in partnership with the Gafsa based 1,000 Volunteers, TTI put on a public conference exhibiting citizen-led initiatives across the city in concert with a city-wide clean up and beautification campaign, thereby both informing the citizenry about how to get involved in their neighborhoods bringing together civil society and government representatives to work together for sustainable solutions.

NEW CONSTITUTION CLUSTER OF ACTIVITIES

As the constitutional drafting process continued to drag on, Tunisians became increasingly dissatisfied with the performance of the government and the Constituent Assembly overall, lacking information on the constitution's articles and their potential impact. In order to urge the

Tunisian women participate in a forum about women's rights in the new constitution

Constituent Assembly to provide information to the electorate on the contents of the constitution, TTI worked with a dynamic youth association to produce a flashmob and online petition giving voice to Tunisians frustrated with the process. Booths were set up in Downtown Tunis where volunteers distributed copies of the constitution to eager passersby, only for them to open the documents and find the contents blank, leading to a wake up call for recipients to play a more active role in the drafting process. The event entitled "Where is the Constitution?" created significant buzz on the web, with online videos being viewed hundreds of thousands of times and broadcasts on television garnering considerable viewership rates.

Women and youth in particular were critical constituencies to provide their input and feedback on the articles' drafting. Although Tunisian women have long enjoyed formal equality with men, there had been debate on women's role in Tunisian society and their rights in the new Constitution. At least partly the result of an organized, effective Tunisian women's movement, the NCA passed articles 20 and 45 of the new Constitution, institutionalizing of women's equality, however the battle for women's rights were far from over. Therefore, TTI identified during the final drafting process the critical timing to empower women and youth to express their views about their place in the future of Tunisia and provide them the means to make their voices heard. TTI provided support for a Women's Day march and rally in Downtown Tunis aimed at ensuring the new constitution would honor existing legal protection for women and promote gender equality, an event which featured speakers, performers and photo exhibitions. Brainstorming on this took place in numerous Café Politiques sponsored by the project, whereby selected youth and their friends engaged with constitutional experts in various cafes throughout Greater Tunis to hold constructive conversations on the role of the constitution and active citizenship. In partnership with the Association of Mouwatana and Tawassol, TTI supported roundtable discussions that gathered Constituent Assembly Commission Chairpersons, experts involved in drafting the Constitution and 50 representatives of associations and civil society activists to open lines of communication between civil society leaders and NCA members and better inform and shape the final drafting process.

Providing information on the actual contents once the draft was completed, via an In Kind grant to Association Citoyenne Tunisienne, a repeat grantee and part of the prominent network of associations "Bus Citoyen," TTI funded seven educational round tables and events on the constitution in seven different governorates throughout the country. Immediately following these dialogues, participants visited places where youth and the electorate congregate (cafes, youth centers, public squares) to discuss and distribute thousands of copies of the draft document and summary guides printed under related TTI activities. TTI also engaged unique awardees such as the Bicycle Club of Ben Arous to hold a constitutional rally across the governorate where youth

cyclists accompanied by civic education professors and constitutional experts provided information about and celebrated the passage of the new constitution, distributing copies of the constitution along the way. In addition to copies of the actual draft document (which is written in Modern Standard Arabic) that were printed and disseminated by TTI to partners throughout the country, TTI also recognized the importance of offering Tunisian speakers direct access to the document in their own language, and further procured thousands of copies of the constitution translated into Tunisian Arabic for the country's native speakers as well as a constitution summary guide that explained the meaning of each separate article.

In Greater Tunis, TTI partnered with Association de la culture et de l'éducation à la citoyenneté, a repeat grantee, to train association members on the constitution and install strategically located constitution tents where legal and constitutional experts to discuss important articles and distribute further copies of the constitution to thousands of individuals. TTI and the Association Tunisienne Pour L'Integrite et la Democratie des Elections, a repeat grantee that notably worked on the monitoring of the NCA election in 2011, TTI hosted a symposium at the National Library for approximately 300 active citizens entitled: "The Constitution, Between Action and Citizen Appropriation," where international and local constitutional experts discussed three main themes: the role of civil society and political actors in the birth of the Constitution; dynamics relevant to the birth of the Constitution; and the citizen as subject and object of the new Constitution.

The project also used mass media to disseminate information, including nationwide town hall radio shows on the constitution with several citizen representatives debating the contents, as well as 16 televised "constitution capsules" entitled Lama Doustouriya covering the essence of the draft constitution's fundamental articles including commentary from both constitutional law experts and average Tunisians on the street. These discrete informational segments were broadcast free on national television and made available online to expand access to this information beyond TV viewers, reaching over 29 million views in total over a two month period of broadcasting and hundreds more during showings at other TTI constitutional activities.

A still from the Lama Doustouriya set

It is within this context that TTI supported an initiative to inform female students on campuses throughout Greater Tunis about their newly ratified Constitution and provide them with ways to engage them in the political process through a Fixed Obligation Grant to the association Women & Leadership which expert advice, logistics and promotional material for 19 round tables in the university campuses on the Constitution. During each roundtable, an expert and moderator explained the importance of the constitution, screened the constitution capsules, and distributed copies of the constitution itself, facilitating open discussion and presenting options for women to engage and participate in the political process through such ways as active participation in CSOs, political parties, activism in communities, advocacy and active citizenship in general. Questionnaires were used to evaluate participants' knowledge of the new constitution, informing closely monitored visits to women's campuses where trained female students would distribute the constitution and related summary guides to facilitate direct interaction and put into practice their newly acquired knowledge.

TELEVISION PROGRAMMING

Information regarding human dignity, equality, freedom, and definitions that ranged from basic notions of democracy to the most crucial issues being debated in the political arena was identified as being vital for Tunisians. As Tunisia progressed towards complete participatory democracy, access to information about concepts that facilitated citizens' understanding and participation in politics was paramount, and TTI identified television programming as an ideal medium through which to disseminate information to audiences of varied backgrounds, interests, demographics and political leanings. One method that proved effective in fostering increased citizen engagement in and enthusiasm for the developing political process was the production of short, well-targeted television spots that explored the issues and imparted information in an accessible way. Young people in particular remained keen television watchers throughout Tunisia and engaging them through a televised competition with associated publicity was one such way to reach this demographic, generating interest and igniting a passion to do more.

Filming of the election capsules

Building on the success of the aforementioned constitution capsules, TTI developed a series of election capsules that explained critical aspects of the elections and ways citizens could participate. The capsules were facilitated by non-partisan constitutional experts who engaged in live discussions with youth on a variety of related topics including the responsibilities of the electorate, types of elections, the electoral process, the ISIE and its role, and registration. Besides the on air broadcast, the segments were also aired on national radio channels and uploaded to various online video sites as well as a dedicated website as part of a strong social media campaign to encourage the contents to go viral.

Additionally, numerous surveys conducted under TTI informed the project as to particular frustrations with the political process and their public manifestations, including the increasingly negative TV and radio content demonstrating the widespread lost interest and disillusionment in the transition process. It is within this context of frustration and highly charged political environment that famous comedians, who had already proven their capacity to transcend the tensions and channel citizens' frustrations throughout Tunisia's recent history, were used to channel simplified political information to citizens through several TV, radio and online sketches. Themes ranged from concepts of the democratic transition (democracy, freedom of speech, political pluralism) to the next steps in the transition (organization of elections, dissolution of the NCA, formation of a new government and peaceful transference of power).

TTI also utilized this format to air televised debates, allowing citizens to air grievances, decrease tensions and have an informed dialogue with politicians on a national platform. Entitled "Is Tunisia on the Right Track?," TTI and the Munathara Association organized constructive debates whereby each political guest was accompanied by a Tunisian citizen who had won a competition by producing a 99 second statement laying out some of their own ideas and perspectives that were eventually posted online on an activity specific blog for which members could vote. Panelists discussed issues of common interest and spoke openly of the challenges at hand, providing logical and rational arguments aimed at convincing others of their point of view and swaying away from violence and intolerance. The debate was broadcast on national television with impact discussions held on the association's website, a specially designed mobile app, Twitter and Facebook.

Looking to reach young people in particular, and through them their extended families and communities, TTI hired a professional Tunisian production firm to design and produce TV capsules based on the popular national character, Hajj Kloof, who used humor to present core

concepts of democracy and methods for citizen participation for radio and television broadcasts, accompanied by social and print media campaigns. The project also developed its own cartoon character, Lahlouba, initially part of an comic book style active citizen guide aimed at school children which provided lessons on democratic principles and scenarios which youth could present and discuss with their parents, and further developed into television spots entitled "Lahlouba Takes Us to the Elections." The activity designed and produced television spots featuring the character explaining critical aspects of the elections and ways for citizen participation, disseminated in partnership with CSOs and accompanied by strong social media coverage in order to introduce new electoral processes to Tunisians across the country. Further targeting the student demographic, the program sought to increase the knowledge and awareness of the constitution and civics through a national televised quiz competition show, partly based on the content presented in the elections and constitution capsules and supported again by strong social media promotion.

Hajj Kloof, above, uses humor to present core concepts of democracy and methods for citizen participation

ACTIVISM TRAINING

A TTI survey about youth political engagement found that young Tunisians perceived that their voices were not heard as loudly or clearly as they should due to lack of capacity to adequately advocate for their needs, as well as an absence of opportunities for them to express themselves non-violently, leading to frustration, disengagement and, in some cases, radicalization. Many participants who were actively engaged at the beginning of the Revolution began disengaging amidst perceptions that the government was being forced on them rather than being something they could shape or influence, leading to ignorance and suspicion of both civil society and government writ large. Encouragingly, while the civil society space was still very nascent, there were many initiatives driven by new associations, activists, and neighborhood groups that were actively engaged in the community. In particular, there was an increased presence of youth-led civil society activism in the transition space following the 2011 elections; these groups sought to connect with their communities in new and innovative ways that spoke to the reality of their respective experiences. While the culture of activism is still young in Tunisia, the growing frustration with top down reform led some local activists to clamor for change and recognize that they must be the agents for this change.

A particularly Tunisian activism approach has been its adoption of "Artivist" engagements, incorporating cultural approaches to traditional activism problems through blogging and slam poetry contests, flash mobs, street art, breakdance, calligraffiti and street art, rap and music training in addition to more structured dialogue such as workshops and roundtables to better engage with their constituencies and subsequently becoming a model for other Arab Spring countries in the creative leadership of young citizens with a stake in their country's future. TTI

Participants at the "Level Up" Artivist workshop meet outside to brainstorm and collaborate

utilized these approaches during a multi-day training in Gafsa designed to increase skills in advocacy techniques among community activists in order to promote citizen engagement. Through an In Kind grant, a consortium of prominent cultural associations in Gafsa organized four iterations of a three day training on how to leverage visual and creative arts to support advocacy efforts for youth activists from Gafsa, an area renowned for visual and creative arts in the interior where many youth groups engaged in the cultural space. The training was both instructional and provided an opportunity for participants to use their various artistic medium

in designing advocacy campaigns in a hands-on training focused on three basic cultural tools in advocacy initiatives: digital culture (including social media), videography and fine arts. Building off this, through an In Kind grant to Jaw Gsarnia, a Kasserine based group of active bloggers, TTI conducted leadership and advocacy skills training for youth bloggers and critics who do not have the appropriate skills to lead community advocacy efforts, emphasizing multimedia engagement in particular and soliciting input from youth in the community before presenting the results to relevant government officials.

In addition to prioritizing the advocacy of youth in general, TTI also sought to increase the voice of female advocates in Tunisia. An event held by prominent Tunisian NGO Woman & Leadership and covered extensively in the national media brought together more than 120 activists, journalists, and opinion shapers to increase awareness of women's roles, rights, and access to resources under the current laws; share their experiences of gender-based violence; and strategize methods to ensure their opinions were heard. Moreover, for interior communities, activism training paired with community meetings and activism open houses in key zones where frustration and dissent were most prominent provided participants with the communication skills for productive government engagement, effective analytical skills to identify the most pressing issues in their communities, and the means to advocate for those issues in order to effect positive change.

As the issues became more complex and the debate became more sophisticated, it was even more important to find effective ways of conducting outreach and promoting youth activism. Similarly, the CSOs themselves needed to continuously grow and adapt to the changing social, technological, and artistic context in order to stay relevant and effective. One way of doing this was to build on the expertise of activists in other countries who have supported or participated in political transitions and can share knowledge and support for CSOs to plan for the future. TTI conducted an activism training workshop entitled "Level Up" which brought together leading Tunisian youth-based CSOs with international experts including the founders of the world renowned digital activism and music Exit Festival to learn, share and develop specific plans for building the network and range of tools available for Tunisian civil society to increase its influence in the transition space. The workshop balanced the fundamentals of building CSO capacity and improving their effectiveness with cutting edge sessions led by acknowledged world experts in campaigning, cybersecurity, web design and game and app creation for change, sustainability, advocacy, whistleblowing, privacy and political activist platforms. Workshop deliverables included action plans for CSO collaboration and networking in the run up to elections, a 'campaign plan' for engaging a wider group of Tunisian CSOs in the youth political engagement movement, design and development of workshops to be implemented at the follow on "BTD Fair," *Joussour*, which was held later that spring.

YOUTH CENTERS AND SPORTING ACTIVITIES

As Tunisia transitioned towards democracy, encouraging young people to find their place in the new social and political landscape was a priority, particularly as extremist groups offered

The new computer equipment provided by TTI at the Youth Center of Medenine

disengaged youth a sense of structure and community. The rate of crime, drug use, and gravitation towards extremist groups was most visible amongst youth who believed that they did not have a place within the new social or political context of their community. Given the lack of structured outlets for young people, activities involving youth centers and sports found particular success in addressing this due to their cross cutting nature, incorporating multiple objectives such as civic engagement, marginalized groups, youth engagement, and CVE. Youth centers served as the central educational, cultural and athletic facilities for young men and women, thereby being the ideal locations to encourage youth in positive civic engagement and show tangible results of the Revolution's achievements.

Participation in athletic activities was a way for young Tunisians to engage in their communities and express themselves as individuals in a positive manner, however access to facilities, training, and equipment was limited. Through an in-kind grant to the Municipality of Kasserine and in collaboration with a group of sports teachers, TTI worked with the city's youth center to provide minor rehabilitation and equipment for an outdoor gym, as well as materials and logistical support for a day of youth obstacle course competitions upon completion of installation of the equipment designed to bring youth from different neighborhoods together to form teams and work together to overcome the challenges. This activity was part of a cluster of activities designed to encourage youth to actively engage in moderate society through athletic and artistic self-expression in partnership with the Ministry of Culture held in Youth Centers throughout the country.

Beyond youth center rehabilitation, TTI also organized a number of competitions and tournaments complete with uniform and equipment provision, as well as professional trainings. A soccer tournament and training

A young girl shows pride at participating in a soccer clinic at a youth center in Kasserine

session for 40 young men from the Sidi El Bechir youth center was held at the stadium in La Marsa, led by famous Tunisian national team coach Mokhtar Tlili and a team of professional referees. The activity's training, tournament and award ceremony were captured through both photos and video, which were later uploaded onto the Youth Center's Facebook page, garnering significant attention and positive response from those associated with the activity as well as other youth centers seeking to emulate the results, underscoring that activities such as these helped to prevent the cycle of violence in at risk youth by providing outlets and avenues for productive engagement and inclusion. In the interior, a two day co-ed ping pong competition demonstrated to youth that a new chapter was being developed in Tunisia's history by providing them a place to learn, play, grow and express themselves free of government repression. Through this event, youth became regulars at the center and enthusiasts of its other activities, thus avoiding inappropriate venues where they might be easy prey for manipulation. Other popular sports that TTI sought to encourage youth participation in include judo and karate training, boxing gym refurbishment, petanque court provision and skate park construction in tandem with extreme sport demonstrations, often featuring well known enthusiasts or champions to serve as role models for the participants.

Youth Centers as Mechanisms for Lasting Change

On the TTI program, youth centers were a means to achieve a wide range of programmatic objectives, including CVE, civic engagement and inclusion of marginalized communities. This cross-cutting methodology was used to support all of the project's sub-objectives, particularly by providing tangible examples of the benefits of the Revolution and democratic change. They helped to identify strong partners, key demographics and inspiration for future activities, linking and building upon earlier successes to achieve greater impact overall.

At the Youth Center of Medenine in southern Tunisia, being an important educational, cultural and athletic center for young people in the area, the project's assistance allowed the center to become the trusted hub of youth activity and accept even more youth who needed a productive way to spend their time outside of school, consequently acquiring information and skills to improve their ability to engage in participatory democracy. At other youth centers and schools, facilities had deteriorated and sporting equipment was lacking, and so through their rehabilitation these activities helped to prevent violence and encourage better relations between students and teachers, as well as young men and women in their communities.

Beyond athletic facilities, youth centers also provided organized classes and computer labs with internet access, as well as occasional vocational training for young attendees. Numerous activities addressed tensions of students following violence in the interior which had resulted in frustration and delinquency, as well as destruction and theft of school property in some cases, assessing procurement needs such as for IT equipment, meeting room furniture and AC units, bringing together students, their families and teachers to help adequately prepare for school attendance and exams. They were also the ideal locations to host community events, such as celebrations of national holidays like Republic Day or the anniversary of the Revolution, building feelings of unity amongst youth and reviving the spirit of hope in the Revolution in order to support the democratic transition process. Activities provided material support for the celebrations, including banners, Tunisian flags, symbolic gifts and t-shirts emblazoned with constructive slogans to encourage youth to continue to support their Revolution through intellectual, sporting and entertainment activities and cultural performances.

TOLERANCE AND NON-VIOLENT COMMUNICATION

Political debate and public exchange of opinions that would have been silenced during the previous regime were hallmarks of post-Revolution Tunisia; despite these positive developments, intolerance marked by violence also surfaced. It was at this juncture in Tunisian history that there was a need to focus on national unity and the engrained acceptance of tolerance in Tunisian identity. Tunisia's rich heritage is a testimony to the benefits of tolerance and diversity, and inspiring Tunisians to forge a future based on a shared national identity was an essential programming goal throughout the life of the project. Many of these initiatives were quick response or entry activities which allowed the program to work with new partners and/or new areas, or served as precursors to CVE activities which helped identify key target groups, possible activity responses and target areas.

TTI partnered with local organization "Association de la culture et de l'education a la citoyennete" to implement a two-phased tolerance awareness program targeting Tunis and Gafsa residents. The first phase began with writing competitions and a series of painting workshops which took place at four universities in the Tunis metro area, as well as secondary schools in Tunis and Gafsa. The second phase featured a public "tolerance awareness tent" display which was assembled on two separate days in high visibility locations in the Tunis metro area to engage with citizens and encourage tolerance and anti-violence measures. In the interior, the project's Sbeitla office collected stories around the theme of inter-tribal collaboration and shared them with the community in Gafsa to help rebuild bridges in the historically tolerant and pluralistic region which, following the Revolution, had become riven along tribal lines giving rise to violence and suspicion. Participants agreed that the story collecting and sharing with tribal elders from different delegations across the governorate helped the conflicted community deal more openly with the troubling trend of tribalism which obscured real issues and threatened community cohesion through laughs and lessons shared among the different generations.

Targeting students in particular, the program brought together university students with diverging points of view to participate in an inclusive forum with open and civil dialogue looking for sources of unity between and among the participants. The discussions were accompanied by campus awareness campaigns to further disseminate constructive messages in their respective universities and help restructure the student movement to ensure continued positive involvement in the transition.

A billboard in Montplaisir featuring the
"We Are Different, But Without Conflict" campaign

As a way to reinvigorate the spirit of unity and peace nationwide, TTI in partnership with local media firm Panorama designed a series of striking images of mosaicked male and female faces, respectively, representing the diversity of Tunisian identities and displayed on billboards, bus shelters and store fronts declaring "We Are Different, But Without Conflict," promoting tolerance and acceptance of diverse viewpoints as part of the democratic transition. These traditional print media productions were supplemented by prime time TV and radio spots, a "Tous Tolerants" Facebook page and viral videos depicting Tunisians' reactions when looking in a bathroom mirror, but seeing that a different person was holding the tolerance slogan on a sign, garnering thousands of views, likes and shares going beyond the close of the activity. Due to its success, TTI undertook a follow on activity using the same imagery but declaring "Listen to Me, Don't Reject Me." Similar to the earlier activities, this imagery was featured on billboards throughout TTI's seven governorates as well as throughout prominent social media sites, national radio airtime, and guest spots on the country's most popular television shows, reaching an estimated 2.5 million Tunisians. Responses were overwhelmingly popular, with viewers commenting about the value of the message and the importance of listening to other peoples' points of view as an inherently Tunisian value.

The project also utilized radio and television broadcasting in its partnership with the El Masna organization and the well known Tunisian singer Bayrem Kilani, widely known as "Bendir Man," to bring together a group of young Tunisian musicians, singers and artists to promote the values of tolerance and pluralism through their creation of a collaborative song and music video entitled "Ghena Lik," or "A Song for You." The song's lyrics encouraged all Tunisians to keep their country in their hearts and stay faithful to the struggle for reform, with the accompanying video featuring the diverse people and scenery of the country along with artistic depictions of the tolerant Tunisian identity. The song and video debuted live on Tunisian radio and television stations just days

On set during the Ghena Lik music video shoot
with Bendir Man

before anniversary of the 2011 Constituent Assembly elections. All artists involved in the production were interviewed about the work, which received acclaim from both the national and international press, reaching number one in the Tunisian billboard charts.

The use of new technology to highlight Tunisian culture and history was utilized as a way to bring the past to life as well as to sustain positive momentum during the transition process. In  order to engage citizens of different cultural, political, and religious backgrounds, TTI partnered with a local organization to produce and present a laser graphic display at two locations: one on the Avenue Habib Bourguiba (the main boulevard of Tunis), and the other in the interior city of Gafsa at the Centre des Arts Dramatiques et Scéniques. The production depicted an enthralling chronology of Tunisia's pluralistic history and was free for all people in attendance to enjoy, as were the more than 1,500 Tunisian flags distributed at the venue in order to give people a physical symbol of unity.

The results of these tolerance activities and others were reviewed and analyzed for effectiveness and resonance by local survey firm, Prodata, whose findings among young men and women between the ages of 18 and 27 who participated in the focus groups showed that respondents appreciated the originality of the campaign and its consistency across the various media, remarking that the work reminded people of the historical tolerance present in Tunisia and the positive times when citizens came together in support of the Revolution.

COUNTERING VIOLENT EXTREMISM

In the interior of Tunisia and select areas of Greater Tunis where poverty and lack of economic opportunity overlap, extremist groups offered the feeling of affiliation and involvement to vulnerable people at a time when there were few constructive outlets. The rate of crime, drug use, and gravitation towards extremist groups is most visible amongst youth who believe that they do not have a place within the new social or political context of their community. Unemployment, a sense of hopelessness, lack of faith that the political process will yield any meaningful change, and an absence of worthwhile past times or social outlets reinforced the sense of alienation and disconnection from Tunisian society felt by young people. There was a clear need to attract young people and engage them in platforms for expression, new ideas, and inclusive activities to counter the spread of violence and create a sense of belonging.

TTI aimed to reinforce youths' sense of belonging to moderate Tunisian society by the presentation of interesting, "cool" alternate pursuits that establish strong, influential moderate peer groups and foster pride in community as a powerful antidote to many of the 'push-pull' factors that draw young people to extremism. These activities ranged from hosting street art workshops teaching such skills like calligraffiti to hip hop and breakdance trainings to music festivals with national and internationally renowned artists and performers such as were held in the Thakafa Manifesto and Joussour activities. These events usually also featured roundtable discussions and breakout groups with the at risk youth in order to give participants the opportunity to network with like-minded individuals and express themselves in a constructive manner, thereby providing an outlet for alternative expression. The program focused on the demographic most vulnerable to joining violent extremist efforts in Tunisia, being 15-35 year old males from urban areas and rural population centers. Programming occurred in two principle locations: Greater Tunis (Ettadhamen in Ariana governorate; Douar Hicher in Manouba governorate; Al Intilaka, Sidi El Béchir and Sijoumi in Tunis governorate) and the governorate of Kasserine (Kasserine Nord and Ezzahour).

Arts were also a mechanism to build the sense of belonging for youth at-risk of joining extremist groups. In Kasserine, TTI designed an activity entitled "Kasserine's Got Talent!" to increase confidence among youth to enable them to express themselves creatively and strengthen their sense of belonging through the holding of a governorate-wide talent production. The activity supported the casting and selection process for youth in various performance arts, as well as a workshop that focused on confidence building and a large final performance for the best youth performers. In order to recruit participants, the awardee worked with individual youth centers and a team of twelve expert coaches, the Ministry of Youth and Sports and the Regional Directorate of Kasserine to organize outreach

Competitors in "Kasserine's Got Talent!"

and auditions among youth in vulnerable communities were there was a high incidence of criminality and appeal to extremist groups. These individuals received training in hip hop/rap, traditional music performance, break dancing, theater and musical instrumentation as well as civic engagement before taking part in a final performance which was filmed and shared with national television, radio, print journalism and online media, demonstrating that there were many individuals with shared interests in the arts who could come together for support and community to build their confidence before a public audience and take part in extracurricular activities that showcased their talents.

Elsewhere throughout the country, workshops were held in targeted areas focusing on youth between the ages of 14 - 23 by providing instruction on hip hop, breakdance, fine arts, theater and youth civic education skills, where participants were exposed to some basic civic engagement ideas that they were then encouraged to incorporate in their selected artistic discipline. The final performances not only provided youth with the opportunity to showcase their talents, connect with their peers, but additionally to instill pride among marginalized youth while performing on a national stage.

TTI used both the arts and sports to provide engagement. Sports activities often linked tangible and event-based programming, for example focusing on community building with school or youth center cleaning and rehabilitation followed by sports camps or competitions designed to bring disparate at risk youth and their families together with teachers and community leaders in a positive context. Often these engagements also supported the founding of certain youth athletic clubs by bringing nationally recognized athletes to encourage youth to form structured teams that could continue to engage with young people from other at risk neighborhoods after the close of the activity, such as through street basketball teams, skateboarding crews or amateur boxing clubs.

Street theater was also conducted in partnership with repeat TTI awardee Fani Raghman Anni, performing numerous plays on the topics of moderation and tolerance in vulnerable neighborhoods throughout Greater Tunis, incorporating local community members in the preparation and performance of the activities in order to counteract the inherent mistrust and volatile security situation present there, ensuring greater acceptance and a transference of capacities to community members who could then be involved in future activities in the area. Street dance performances like those organized with YEDA were likewise undertaken to "kick out the violence" and demonstrate alternative methods of self expression, starting with workshops and rehearsals led by professional dancers followed by public performances and discussions on social responsibility and leadership cultivation.

A skateboarding park built by TTI in Kasserine

The development of youth leaders and role models in general proved a strong method of counteracting the pull of extremist groups and influencing their peers to espouse moderation and participation in mainstream social and political outlets. Trainings to cultivate leadership skills and foster a sense of belonging to moderate society focused on building relations with at-risk youth; proactive dialogue; skills of a community leader and influencer; networking to find the right partners and credible voices in the community to reach youth at risk; researching their own community to locate resources; and interactive and creative approaches to strengthening youth sense of belonging.

In order to better inform and shape the project's CVE activity design and implementation strategy overall, TTI procured the services of Navanti LLC to conduct a baseline assessment of extremism trends in Kasserine and Greater Tunis. Navanti held focus groups and conducted interviews and surveys conducted with males between the ages of 18 to 35 throughout eight representative cities, providing research and reporting that fused national and sector level analysis with on the ground insight from local researchers, CVE experts, and social media data analysis to understand the environmental conditions and dynamics in the specific and focused geographic areas. The assessment covered three topical areas (youth and community perceptions of extremism, youth leadership, and accessing the community and youth demographic) and gathered baseline data on CVE indicators, including level of youth participation in moderate youth organizations, availability of nonviolent means of expression on issues of concern, leadership capacity of youth leaders, trusted sources of information, recreational activities and places of congregation, perceptions of political elites and institutions and programmatic opportunities. The findings from the activity were used to design more targeted and efficacious CVE programming and better assess their impact.

A follow on study was conducted approximately seven months later to assess changes in attitude and perception, as well as the level of awareness of TTI activities and whether that exposure led to changed behavior to minimize susceptibility to extremist influences.

The Kasserine reports had a number of recommendations that were relevant to ongoing and future programming in the interior, such as installing wireless internet access at local youth centers to draw people to constructive activities and networking while also building on the power of social media to disseminate positive messaging; improving gym facilities to attract "uncultivated" youth with a pre-existing propensity for violence who are unlikely to attend youth center events; and utilize crowd sourced social media sites to counter violent narratives and suggest grassroots solutions. The Greater Tunis reports were also relevant to programming, though they featured a much more broad based view about extremism's roots in Tunisia, looking particularly at Salafism and Ansar Al Shariah, finding that they appealed to certain youth who find it a favorable avenue to express their Muslim identity. Points of contact between young people and Salafist activists included a range of public and private venues frequented by youth, giving the movement easy access to potential recruits, particularly amount working class or impoverished rural areas. Furthermore, American hip-hop culture appeared to resonate with Tunisian youth who saw this as a form of self expression along with other organized activities such as sports leagues. The analysis partly reflected similar (though far less specific) conclusions arrived at in the OTI desktop study that underpinned the development of the CVE strategy.

TTI capitalized on these recommendations in various ways, particularly in the design and strategy of other CVE activities. Specifically, the findings confirmed that TTI had been picking the right types of activities (being music, arts, and sport based) in order to provide a credible alternative to the pull of Ansar al Sharia in particular in light of their methodologies and target recruitment. Furthermore, the reports confirmed the neighborhoods TTI had targeted with its CVE activities were indeed particularly vulnerable and therefore where the project ought to continue to center its CVE activities. The reports additionally provided more evidence to explain how to cultivate a sense of belonging to moderate society among at risk populations, thereby better informing and justifying the beneficiaries chosen and approaches suggested for the project's CVE activities, such as through the project's various youth center activities. Lastly, while the project had been countering Ansar al Sharia's recruitment methods through its art, sport and music activities, the report pointed out that their activities had moved beyond this to include direct political promotion, which TTI had not yet fully incorporated, and therefore took this into consideration with its strategic approach.

MARGINALIZED GROUPS

The disengagement of women, young people and rural dwellers from public affairs allowed Ben Ali to remain in power for 23 years. Public discourse in Tunisia is still not reflective of its demographic makeup. Despite the many achievements Tunisia has made toward democracy and women's rights, as well as the benefits of greater internet penetration in giving a voice to underrepresented groups, much of the public discourse in the country is still dominated by older adult males. As such, these groups were key target populations for TTI programming across its various sub-objectives because of their seminal role in driving the political activism that led to the downfall of the dictator. That experience notwithstanding, the concept of free political expression was still a novel concept, and engaging marginalized groups in constructive political dialogue was a key program objective. By creating venues for political expression, TTI aimed to alleviate frustration over lingering political and economic issues in constructive ways for marginalized groups.

Transferring political energy into voter participation was an exemplary challenge for post Revolution Tunisia, where young Tunisians instrumental in the events of the Revolution and first election began to lose interest and momentum in the transition process. TTI worked with the Association of Young Leaders and Entrepreneurs, a youth mentorship group, to develop a two phased activity aimed at increasing participation of young Tunisians in the voting process entitled "Countdown: Build Tunisia in 20 Hours." The first phase began as a three day workshop on the theme of how to get Tunisian youth to vote where project development and presentations

were undertaken by the 100 participants, culminating in a marathon 20 hour work session. In the second phase, teams exhibited their proposals to a panel of judges and attendees, the best of which were selected to be funded and executed by the project. Due to the success of the initial event in Tunis, a subsequent activity was undertaken in the interior, whereupon 60 youth from Kasserine, Sidi Bouzid and El Kef were joined by 20 youth activists from the region to develop projects that ranged from "Rock the Vote" inspired concerts to voter education buses and pop up dance shows to attract youth to places where voter information would be distributed. YLE collected all proposals from both events and shared them throughout their donor network, helping to ensure the youth continued to work on identifying opportunities to make these projects viable.

Youth needed to demonstrate not only to political leaders but also to their peers the important role that they played in the Revolution and subsequent transition process in order to maintain their momentum and involvement. Through a grant to the Andalus Institution of Tolerance and Anti-Violence Studies, TTI produced a video documentary showcasing youth leadership and voices in the interior, then hosted a series of screenings throughout the area. In addition, TTI conducted a documentary training in both Tunis and Kasserine, entitled "Zoom Into My Country." Selected amateur youth videographers received training in videography and documentary filmmaking, eventually producing four films which captured youth leadership and participation through the lens of: the role and influence of local culture, the important economic and social role that given areas have on the interior, ways in which the government is preserving local monuments and how to improve, and a review of the production of charcoal and its environmental impact.

Youth enjoying musical performances at the Thakafa Manifesto Festival, a cross cutting activity designed to positively engage participants as part of the project's suite of youth CVE programming

To demonstrate this to wider audiences and bring together TTI's various artistic endeavors, the project organized a number of street art and activism festivals, such as the Thakafa Manifesto which featured activism and arts training, photo exhibitions, cultural seminars and debates, free expression spaces for performance artists, calligraffiti shows, theater scenes and dance exhibitions all held in downtown Tunis on the Avenue Habib Bourgiba targeting marginalized communities for engagement and countering violent extremism. The project helped develop festival websites, Facebook pages and YouTube channels to encourage networking, peer connections and information sharing among the disparate groups in attendance from throughout the country, proving an ideal forum for conflict management and advocacy.

TTI partnered with the Sbeitla Women's Committee as well as the municipality of Sbeitla to create a safe community park for female residents of neighborhoods which had been fraught by youth delinquency and violence. This activity provided an opportunity to rebuild relationships between youth, the municipality, and support the important role that this women's committee played in safeguarding its community. The objective of this partnership was to support the creation of a community space that was open and safe for women and families to use, as well as open channels of constructive communication between the community and the local municipality, sowing the seeds of trust between the community and the local government.

The One Billion Rising For Justice activity combined numerous means of artistic expression in order to bring awareness of the importance of women's participation in the political process and gender equality while discouraging violence and marginalization. The event included a flashmob, dancing and street theater performances, and projections of select films to demand an end to violence against women and to make a stand for women's empowerment.

To increase youth and female voices specifically in the political space, TTI partnered with repeat awardee the Munathara Association to hold a series of debates focusing on Tunisia's transition to democracy and stemming from a competition among Tunisian youth which were televised and broadcast online in addition to being tracked through social media, contributing to greater diversity in public opinion and encouragement of political dialogue through a multitude of forums. Building on the success found by publicizing marginalized viewpoints through this debate series, TTI in partnership with the Sawty Association also produced and viralized a video ahead of the October 23rd elections anniversary demonstrating the concerns of youth from seven different governorates and providing a forum for government officials to answer said concerns, fostering a constructive dialogue and informing both sides of the opinions, challenges and interests of the other.

FOCUS ON THE INTERIOR

While the spirit of the Revolution was embraced throughout the country, its catalyst occurred first in the interior, and as such its residents were extremely proud of their contributions and eager to build on their initial successes. Due however to a relative lack of economic opportunities, a more disengaged and polarized political environment and a largely disempowered or marginalized youth and female demographics leading to a higher prevalence of extremist actors, programming in the interior presented both a challenge to TTI and an opportunity to more fully disseminate its message to critical communities and achieve lasting impact, especially as the project was essentially the only major donor program acting in the interior at all.

As such, the project from the beginning decided to prioritize the importance of activities in the interior, opening an office in July 2011 in Sbeitla, a city at the heart of the interior's most vulnerable and catalytical areas of Gafsa, Kasserine and Sidi Bouzid. The main issues identified for action ranged from frustration over unemployment and unfair distribution of resources, a lack of civic engagement and political participation (especially among the area's roughly 50,000 university students), lack of access to information about political processes or parties, and rural women and youth's marginalization. To address these problems, TTI developed a variety of programming responses for each beneficiary group and sub-objective. In response to concerns about mining delegations and lack of economic opportunity, TTI created workshops to address conflict mitigation, organized forums to bring citizens' concerns to the forefront of government attention, increased advocacy skills so that activism could be more impactful, and undertook messaging and community action campaigns to demonstrate tangible change for frustrated communities. Lessons learned throughout the project confirmed that use of theater and youth focused art groups capitalized on existing art and youth culture scenes, helping to target and engage key groups such as CSOs, university students and bloggers to create effective platforms and networks for programming.

This was especially the case when undertaking CVE activities, given the rise in extremism in the interior in the years following the fall of the previous regime. The interior especially experienced a rise in criminality and drug trafficking as well as a decline in personal security, due in part to a lack of communication between the government and its citizens, which was compounded by a dearth of outlets to help decrease frustrations or voice their concerns about society and politics, especially for youth and particularly in the areas of culture, the arts and sports. TTI activities were designed to mitigate the appeal of extremist ideology and allow citizens to engage in advocating for social, political and economic change, with a particular focus on developing youth to take an active leadership role in civic engagement and activism. Forums, workshops and debate clubs helped bring together interested actors to improve their impact and capacity, while cultural events like hip hop demonstrations, calligraffiti projects and sporting events demonstrated that there existed positive ways to engage within communities outside of extremism with like-minded individuals committed to the success of the transition.

PROGRAMMATIC INNOVATIONS

EFFECTIVE PROGRAMMING THROUGH THE ARTS

Artists of all kinds turned their crafts towards revolutionary subjects following the downfall of Ben Ali both to emulate iconic revolutionary symbols and to explore the complex challenges the country still faced. The Revolution also encouraged a number of artistic manifestos and declarations underscoring the importance of artistic expression and demonstration; artists brought these ideologies to the public through utilization of public fora, reclaiming and reappropriating spaces that used to be controlled solely by the government such as through mural paintings or transforming symbols of the former regime such as police stations or burnt out cars into works of art. Under TTI, the arts were used as a cross cutting theme to reach various target groups rather than as a standalone component, moving beyond entertainment to engage Tunisians culturally with innovative new uses for public theater, art groups, musical performances, expressive dance, cinema production and street art, translating awareness into action by capitalizing on the country's

Tunisian hip-hop dancers performing at the Joussour (Bridges) CSO Fair

existing art and youth culture scenes. The ultimate goal of these activities was to provide cultural opportunities for people to improve their communities, reduce violence through building confidence, and promoting tolerance and positive engagement.

Building upon traditional artistic means of expression and combining with youth culture, several of TTI's activities for community engagement and clean up incorporated "calligraffiti," a public art form combining the beauty of calligraphy with the inspiration of poetry and the visual immediacy of street art. Groups discussed and practiced the art, then spent time painting and interacting with the community and onlookers regarding the murals' messages about the Tunisian peoples' determination for liberty and tolerance; eventually many participants formed their own calligraffiti clubs creating similar murals and taking part in street art festivals throughout the country. Beyond street art, the program also trained individuals in studio art as well as literature, such as through partnership with the Association de la culture et l'education a la citoyennete. This organization conducted trainings and held art competitions at several universities and high schools around the country centered around tolerance themes, the best works of which were chosen for public display in Tunis alongside historians and sociologists who interacted with passersby and distributed handbooks on tolerance as well as copies of the literature created by similarly chosen competition winners to provoke thought and conversation on tolerance.

Video in general proved to resonate particularly well with young Tunisians, especially video feeds made available through online social media and blog sites. There was abundant interest on the part of young people in the interior in capturing footage to tell local stories and expose the workings of the political process using nothing more than basic camera equipment and an internet connection. Though the level of expertise and sophistication continues to develop, working with creative, motivated young people with a demonstrated interest in filmmaking and political communication was a very promising way to engage young people in teaching and leading their peers about the situation and the stakes in the Tunisian political process. The activity entitled "Zoom Into My Country" was designed to support young filmmakers to learn and create short films about the Tunisian political situation and use them as tool to lead their peers. This activity increased the documentary skills of youth in order to increase the voice of youth in the political process, allowing them to share various experiences and encourage dialogue about how to move the Revolution forward peacefully through a training on the techniques of videography and subsequent exhibition of a selection of shorts publicly Kasserine.

These workshops proved singularly successful as means through which to engage marginalized groups and encourage peaceful civic engagement and build the confidence of disenfranchised youth, and as such were utilized in various musical-themed activities which built upon the country's long established traditions of musical expression. TTI designed a number of music based workshops with in-kind instrument and material provision led by nationally famous performers which culminated in public performances incorporating classical and contemporary

A Zoom Into My Country participant films
her take on the Tunisian political transition

influences as well as original song writing as written by the participants in order to include the wider community and establish musical groups that would continue to practice and showcase their talents after the close of the activity. Building upon the popularity of street culture in particular, the project also undertook numerous rap and hip hop producing trainings designed to allow young artists the means to project their frustrations and hopes with the current socio-economic and political conditions in the country. On a more national level, TTI produced tolerance themed songs with nationally recognized singers such as Bendir Man with corresponding music videos featuring street art with revolutionary symbolism to combat the divisive and extreme rhetoric which often overpowered the voice of younger citizens, many of whom were detached from politics; songs were broadcasted nationally online, on popular radio stations and on television, reaching an unparalleled level of popularity and recognition.

Youth throughout the country not only lacked constructive recreational outlets, but particularly those in at-risk communities were vulnerable to recruitment by extremist groups offering a sense of belonging and purpose which TTI sought to counter through a number of initiatives to train youth in creative self expression and civic education. To counter this, TTI offered a set of initiatives to develop their capacities through trainings on breakdancing, hip hop, beatmaking, arts and theater techniques while simultaneously engaging in civic education games and election simulation activities, among others. TTI partnered with well known Tunisian performance artists Hatem Karoui and Ammar Ltifi to implement activities aimed at developing communication skills through the art of slam poetry, an energetic performance medium which blends spoken word poetry and dramatic performance for live audiences. Another exemplary awardee that worked with TTI was Fani Raghman Anni; this CSO group conducted numerous public performances of youth-created visual arts, dance, and theater works in partnership with local at-risk communities, thereby ensuring acceptance of the activities' message as well as successful transference of capacities to community members who could then be involved in future activities in the area. Workshops with young activists throughout the country proved especially successful as participants organically came together after the activities to perform and compete both nationally and internationally, garnering extensive media coverage through traditional media such as Paris Match as well as online social media forums like Facebook and YouTube where participants uploaded videos to share their experiences. One standout group is the Rocking Steps Crew from Kasserine which TTI supported with initial training followed by materials and logistical support for various public civic engagements and competitions with freestyle rap and "bbop" between dance crew performances to demonstrate for youth in the interior as well as the Ministry of Culture writ large that there are ways that youth can express themselves which are constructive, creative, fun and inclusive.

USE OF SOCIAL MEDIA

In light of the dramatic changes that set in motion the revolutionary protests and eventual ousting of former President Ben Ali, it became evident that new media was playing a key role in maintaining the revolutionary momentum and bringing the voices of disengaged Tunisian youth to the attention of the international community. Satellite technology, cell phones, blogs, YouTube, Facebook and Twitter feeds became instrumental in providing live coverage of protests and speeches as well as platforms for expressing public opinion, bringing an immediacy and human touch to the unfolding events though the coverage that average Tunisians were able to provide after years of government press censorship. Tens of thousands joined Facebook groups that spread independent news and mobilized citizen action, thereby precluding the protests from being hijacked by overly partisan interests, also helped by the fact that students and professionals led the way, followed only after by trade unions and political parties. Bloggers proved that individuals could counter the narrative of state owned media and self-censored newspapers and radio stations, providing alternate views on the events of the day and influencing on a national scale the opinions of average Tunisians. Twitter was used to organize public demonstrations and voice concerns on a large scale when curfew and other government measures sought to curtail freedom of speech, while on YouTube activists shared inspirational rap videos and clips of police brutality during protests that quickly went viral to further fan the revolutionary flames.

This ingratiation of new media and the Revolution demonstrated not only a dependency on these technologies, but also an opportunity to capitalize on the country's capacity, familiarity and literacy with these methods to further stabilization efforts. In order to stay ahead of the curve, the project consulted with other campaigners and monitored trends, including those on Facebook, Twitter, local news, and high school and college campuses, incorporating elements of new media into all projects, not just as stand alone efforts. Furthermore, viral campaigns and online activism proved effective means through which to encourage small CSOs to achieve large impact with training and minimal funding, creating greater resiliency in terms of activity impacts as well as the sustainability of these groups to continue and grow beyond the end of the project. Individual activities as well as organizations were encouraged to create specific Facebook pages, with more developed CSOs receiving additional training in how best to utilize these resources for maximum efficacy. In addition to utilizing new media for activity design and implementation, these sites were used to monitor and evaluate activities during and after completion, being repositories for anecdotal evidence, evidentiary photographs, and communities of like-minded individuals to whom the project could reach out for future activities.

To that end, TTI initiated a number of activities designed to increase new media's capacity to report objectively, including training and workshops for journalists, roundtables involving reporters and activists, blogger to blogger network creation to monitor developments on the constitutional process and incorporation of social media components in all education and awareness raising campaigns. The project also organized public events where TTI-trained journalists demonstrated the skills they acquired during trainings and created actions where bloggers could use social networks to reach other TTI sub-objectives, linking activities and building capacity.

Beyond activities directed at news coverage, TTI also initiated activities which sought to increase citizens' access to and demand for objective information on government and political processes through the medium of social networks, thereby increasing transparency and trust in the government. In both Tunis and Sbeitla program teams managed awareness raising and information dissemination grants on such topics as the constitutional process and its role and impact in a democracy, democratic citizen values, voter education and GOTV efforts, diversity and tolerance, community engagement and anti-violence, incorporating strong visuals to build brand identity and buzz, and Facebook or Twitter pages to form online communities and track responses and photos.

An early example of one of the most utilized online media that the project leveraged includes those developed by TTI grantee Bus Citoyen. Several media outlets (TV, Radio, Newspaper and magazines) covered activities funded by the program which provided good material before, during and after the elections. The media center was a space that facilitated the work of the ISIE and the release of the election results, becoming an important resource for reliable information dissemination and citizen mobilization. Additionally, some of the activities were live broadcasted on local radio, helping to disseminate the information further and get people outside the event informed instantaneously. Prior to the event starting, awardee members were also interviewed on local radio and took the opportunity to invite people to attend. TTI further learned that visibility of their activities was more ensured when the subjects being discussed locally were debated simultaneously with what is being covered at national level.

These lessons were developed and refined for national tolerance campaigns launched through a variety of media, including billboards, radio spots and television broadcasts whose message was bolstered by the release of several viral videos and a Facebook page. The campaign theme from the original launch was "We Are Different, But Without Conflict," with the follow-on's slogans of "We Are Different, But Must Stay United" and "Listen to Me, Don't Reject Me," consisting of two distinct and recognizable collages of male and female faces, respectively. The amalgamation of images, as well as the slogan itself, was designed to appeal to a wide swath of society, being young and old, religious and secular, modern and traditional, male and female, interior and coastal communities. With this wide a swath of target audiences, the project aimed to increase the campaign's penetration and retention by launching a YouTube video set in a public restroom depicting Tunisians' reactions when looking in a mirror but seeing a different person holding the tolerance slogan sign. The video was viewed thousands of times on YouTube alone, and were subsequently uploaded to Facebook garnering over 20,000 views, 21,000 fans and 20,000 likes, along with further commentary supporting the message of tolerance and inclusivity.

Beyond social media, the project also successfully undertook numerous activities that were implemented purely online, such as with the Munathara Association, a Tunisian NGO that leveraged the internet to instigate public debates on the political transition, thereby enhancing civic engagement. Based on the growing popularity of social media throughout Tunisia, Munathara designed an internet platform to create a more inclusive and representative public discourse by creating more opportunities for open debate among youth and between the populace and their political leaders, developing an avid following throughout the country. Through Munathara, TTI led several online debates on topics ranging from "Is Tunisia on the Right Path?" to "Should Tunisia Separate Religion and the State?" Their weekly Facebook reach when from one million to three million Tunisians, subsequently more than doubling their subscribers from 63,000 to 154,000. In addition, the first of its kind iPhone and Android app was developed which allowed users to upload debate videos directly from their phones and engage through commentary online and follow-on in person outreach workshops.

QUICK RESPONSE PROGRAMMING

A further innovation developed under TTI to provide immediate programming responses to quickly changing political and security environments was its Quick Response Framework, as violent timelines led to changes in programming objectives or the need to increase certain ongoing activities in response. While quick response programming occurred throughout the project, TTI's SST developed a specific range of activities that could be adapted to effect immediate impact in the aftermath of high profile violent events or political shifts, often incorporating DDGS elements that could provide visual reinforcement of their calls for tolerance and anti-violence. Activities furthermore were sequenced to make the best use of resources and maximize impact, linking events together under the umbrella of a strong brand to create a network of participants that could go on to further disseminate the peaceful discourse.

An early example of this type of programming was established in response to the Sidi Bouzid shoot out in May 2012. Sidi Bouzid had been a flashpoint between different interest groups, particularly religious conservatives and secularists, which came to a head when the former threatened to shut down commercial businesses that supported the sale of alcohol. Feeling their livelihoods threatened, the business community responded to these threats with violence, leading to retaliation with businesses and trucks in the community being destroyed. TTI sought to diminish tensions with an awareness campaign using the slogan, "Be a Piece of the Solution," displayed on t-shirts, hats and key chains, encouraging citizens to express their opinions constructively, be productive members of their communities, and engage peacefully in the democratic process.

Similarly, in an effort to rebuild community cohesion after the violent clashes between protesters and police forces in Siliana brought on by a perceived lack of government development in the area, CSO activists identified the necessity of fostering open dialogue between citizens and the government in an initiative to find common ground between the two sides that could lead to resolution of the impoverished area's social and economic issues. To support these efforts immediately afterwards, TTI partnered with local associations on an awareness campaign to promote peaceful and constructive dialogue by facilitating a two day interactive form and series of workshops on the state of development in the governorate. To supplement this, the project also engaged the assistance of twenty activists to distribute 5,000 t-shirts, 20,000 stickers and 20 banners emblazoned with the slogan, "I am Siliana, I love Siliana" in coffee shops, school yards, souqs and even police stations to appeal to Tunisians of all ages and demographic groups. Recipients commented that the initiative drew people together after the traumatic event that had started to divide the community along ideological lines.

"I Am Siliana, I Love Siliana"

Following the assassination in February 2013 of opposition politician Chokri Belaid and subsequent mass protests throughout the country, TTI quickly responded in an effort to deescalate tension with positive messages of unity with 15,000 t-shirts, 30,000 stickers and 20 banners featuring anti-violence slogans distributed to sensitive areas with a high level of risk for violence, helping to create a sense of community and solidarity. TTI's response measures were further developed after the second high level political assassination of that year occurred in July with the death of Mohamed Brahmi, where through a quick-response DDGS TTI procured the services of a Tunis-based videographer to capture footage of the demonstrations, recording a key moment in Tunisia's transition to serve as a lesson for future generations. The program also procured and distributed school bags with the words and messaging of its popular "We Are Different But Must Stay United" tolerance campaign to school children in youth centers from at-risk neighborhoods throughout Greater Tunis, spreading the message to students, their families and neighbors, further building on the established brand identity. Additionally, TTI adapted already ongoing programming begun in June of that year with a street festival and public laser light mapping projection show displayed a month after the assassination in Downtown Tunis and later Kasserine visually displaying the history of Tunisia starting from pre-history through the Punic eras and Islamic civilizations to the present day Republic as characterized by tolerance, moderation, hospitality and rejection of violence. The use of this new technology to highlight Tunisian culture and history was a way to bring the past to life, as well as to sustain positive momentum during the change process in order to engage citizens of different cultural, political, and religious backgrounds around a common theme of unity.

PROGRAM OPERATIONS

STAFFING

All positions essential to implementing the TTI contract based on the initial funding ceiling and expected program levels were filled by the end of September 2011, including the regional office in Sbeitla which was opened in late July 2011. Following discussion with the Senior Management Team, steps were taken to expand the project staff by the addition of two activity teams comprising a Program Development Officer (PDO), a Grant manager (GM) and Procurement and Logistics Officer (PLO), one in each office. The Sbeitla Office was initially led by a national Head of Field Office and a short term expat program manager, a position which converted to a long term position in May of 2012. This position was required as in addition to the complexity of OTI grant writing in general, the staff there struggled with producing their grants in English, and this position addressed the gap in capacity and helped to achieve higher and faster grant clearance. The position was retitled "Regional Program Manager" in March 2013 to be consistent with OTI conventions.

The initial COP and Operations Manager departed from their respective positions in April of 2012, with the former Sbeitla Regional Program Manager assuming the position of COP and a new Operations Manager joining the team from DAI Home Office. The new team instituted a number of procedural and administrative changes but were not able to meet the dynamic needs of the program, and left their positions in December and January respectively. A new Acting COP was selected in December, and was approved to take on the position full time in January 2013; supported by OTI and the DAI Home Office project manager, DAI undertook significant restructuring, plus recruitment and training of national staff in order to improve program effectiveness. A new Operations Manager arrived in March 2013.

A surge in terms of national staffing was undertaken to achieve a commensurate increase in implementation capacity, also allowing additional flexibility to program and disburse additional funds to better meet program goals. This surge was coupled with a reorganization and streamlining of management responsibilities, with the organizational chart rationalized to minimize the number of direct reports of any one supervisor, thereby allowing adequate time for supervision and mentorship, as well as empowerment among the Tunisian managers and fostering pride of program ownership. When the new Country Representative arrived in April 2013 this was significantly strengthened through the creation of a Senior Strategy Team comprised of expat and Tunisian team leaders to inform project strategy development foster Tunisian ownership, as well as comprehensive and redeveloped Performance Management Plan reviews as a key management tool to reinforce roles and responsibilities while also allowing for constructive and engaging staff development and dialogue.

One key position filled after an extended vacancy was the vital post of office manager to make significant inroads into rationalizing and managing project resources. This post had initially been created to manage only the Tunis office, but the scope was expanded to include standardization of administrative procedures between both offices when appropriate.

An additional staffing challenge arose as a consequence of the September 14, 2012 attack on the US Embassy, after which the number of in-country OTI positions was decreased from two slots to one. The loss of the Deputy Country Representative (DCR) post initially left a notable gap in a number of key functions such as grant development, M&E and reporting, and contributions to strategic development, in addition to the normal OTI review functions in the TTI activity cycle. At the February 2013 Four Corners meeting, OTI and DAI developed a joint scope of work for a TTI DCOP-Programs whose position was designed to shoulder many of the programmatic functions previously performed by the DCR and closely collaborate with the CR on program issues. This position was filled in May 2013, however it was eventually decided that the skill sets identified in the scope of work did not sufficiently address the needs of the program and the position was vacated in October 2013. While this experience did not result in lasting success, it was instructive in terms of lessons learned for identifying best fit candidates for certain positions, and therefore a DCOP-Programs with a more suitable skillset to the SOW could still be effective in other OTI contexts. After the departure of the DCOP-P, the challenges inherent in the limited USG staffing footprint were overcome through even greater prioritization of collaborative and open communication between the Country Representative and TTI team that had already been put in place to good effect, establishing an ongoing and deep involvement in all aspects of the program. The in-country team also significantly simplified the activity cycle to reflect the single OTI reviewer in the "concept to cleared" cycle, and made better use of the OTI Program Management Assistant for grant administration and records maintenance. The addition of an expatriate independent consultant Information officer in November 2013 to draft routine reports and snapshots was significant value add to the program and greatly streamlined the important reporting and information aspects of the program.

As the end of the period of performance approached in the fall of 2013, the recruitment and retention of national staff became a more prominent issue of concern. Under Tunisian labor law, TTI was obliged to offer defined duration contracts, as hiring employees on open ended bases required costly payouts at project completion. As closedown loomed, staff began to seek other opportunities in order to avoid periods of unemployment, however with a period of performance of less than a year, a difficulty arose in recruiting staff for short duration contracts in response to vacancies. In order to avoid attrition and retention problems, TTI therefore requested and was subsequently granted approval to offer retention payments to staff commensurate with one month salary for each year of their involvement in the project, which was critical to the successful closedown of the project. Additionally a number of key staff who won new positions before the end of the program period of performance nonetheless negotiated transitions that minimized hardship for the programming and allowed effective management of the workload.

FINANCE

Reinforced finance guidance and training proved the key to successful financial management of the TTI project. Despite initial issues in terms of some of the procedures for financial processing and tracking, additional formalized training and restructuring of responsibilities ensured better efficiencies and administration of project finances in the field during Phase Two, which were further solidified under Phase Three. In addition, many aspects of program administration and grant implementation that had been hampered by extended turnaround times for processing of financial transactions were expedited with a redesign of the project finance and administration arrangements from the ground up.

DAI Home Office provided extended STTA finance support that revamped and systematized the project financial system, and provided extensive training for finance staff and project management in DAI's Field Accounting System, which yielded dramatic improvements in financial performance and responsiveness. Importantly, OTI approved the addition of a Human Resources Assistant to the staff, which allowed a member of the finance team who had also been attending to HR administration to focus on accounting full-time. Program administration, finance, and procurement became increasingly efficient and responsive to project priorities in light of the rollout of the Field Operations Manual and the training period for surge staff that was extended to existing staff to ensure uniformity. The previous organizational structure, in which the COP had numerous direct reports and the Director of Finance had numerous administrative and procurement responsibilities, partly explained procurement and project administration inefficiencies. The revised structure freed the Director of Finance to focus on management and leadership of the project finance function exclusively, again allowing for improved functionality.

Given the surge in staff and resulting increase in implementation capacity in anticipation of more ambitious grant targets during that period, the OTI-DAI response was to clarify the shared picture of the project's remaining obligation and expectations for additional funds. In March and April, TTI staff were able to focus intensively on grant closeout and de-obligation in order to determine how much remains available for programming. Based on this clearer picture, TTI was much better placed to plan the spending of confirmed and anticipated funds. Two subsequent obligation increases as well as a budget realignment brought these expectations into alignment with program implementation, and regular Financial Four Corners meetings helped ensure all members of the team shared the same understanding and expectations regarding the project's finances.

SECURITY

Despite the relatively peaceful transfer of power from the former regime to the National Constituent Assembly, instability remained and instances of civil unrest emerged sporadically, occasionally descending into violence. While the vast majority of anti-government protests occurred in central Tunis, violent incidents especially in the interior fueled fears of extremism at odds with Tunisia's historical abhorrence of violence as a means of achieving political transition. As initial incidents occurred largely spontaneously, in certain instances the unrest and violence led authorities to impose curfews on the citizenry as a means of controlling and decreasing manifestations of popular discontent.

Rural areas of Tunisia have long been affected by poverty and unemployment, and many of the foreign mining firms that account for much of the local economy had yet to return after leaving during the uprising. As a result, competition over jobs became fierce, occasionally leading to violent clashes. In Tunis, most demonstrations bemoaned the slow pace of political and economic reforms since Ben Ali's departure, as well as fears that former regime officials may return to power. Cases of crimes against properties and/or persons decreased significantly from the immediate post-Revolution period, but a new form of violence aimed at undermining fundamental freedoms of citizens to express themselves, to dress or the freedom of media emerged from the Salafists as a result of the opening of the political space.

As the Country Representative was out of the country following the attack on the US Embassy in September 2012, DAI management did not have immediate access to an Embassy or OTI point of contact to seek advice about the changing situation on the ground in Tunis. The subsequent Country Representative then brokered a meeting for the COP with the Embassy Regional Security Officer (RSO) in order to discuss the security picture and courses of action in event of future emergencies, which greatly facilitated TTI's ability to react and respond to changing security contexts. Though the Country Representative remained TTI's principal point of contact, in the event that she was not available, the COP's ability to contact the RSO directly in emergencies provided another layer of confidence about program security. To supplement this, a DAI Security Specialist visited TTI in October to create a Business Continuity Plan, evaluate physical security of both the Tunis and Sbeitla offices, and to review the project security policies and procedures.

TTI implemented all practicable recommendations of the DAI Home Office review of security in its Sbeitla and Tunis offices, notably upgrades to the physical security measures of both offices, and improved access controls. In response to concerns about Sbeitla office security and in the aftermath of a break-in, TTI rented the only remaining vacant suite in the Sbeitla building in order to prevent it being rented by another tenant, and recruited an additional night watchman. The newly appointed office manager assumed the role of Security Focal Point for all program security measures and has established contact with DAI Home Office security in order to follow up directly on matters of security concern. The COP and Operations Manager also made concerted efforts to network with Tunis-based security personnel from other projects and firms in order to stay abreast of the changing security situation.

The demonstrations in the aftermath of the Belaid and Brahmi assassinations and associated movement restrictions caused some disruption to normal program activities, though this was generally overcome with "work from home" arrangements. Tunisian staff made a concerted effort to keep project management apprised of the changing situation on the ground, and updates relayed via email and text to the Country Representative were well-received and relayed to OTI-Washington as appropriate. In the event of office closures, the phone tree and warden system worked effectively.

Security also became a greater concern during this period, particularly in the interior. Tunisian security forces waged a prolonged crackdown on extremists operating out of Mount Chaambi, not far from the Sbeitla program office. The atmosphere of fear and uncertainty, and occasional movement restrictions, had a moderate impact on TTI's ability to program in the interior. TTI used the downturn as an opportunity to review and revise its information sharing, movement and security protocols. Project management continued to watch the situation closely, keeping staff apprised of changes, and reviewing programming decisions on a routine basis. TTI field staff also continued to exercise the same cultural sensitivity and community engagement that had been a hallmark of programming in the interior, affording the program team a high degree of local acceptance and community buy-in.

BEST PRACTICES AND LESSONS LEARNED

FLEXIBLE STRATEGIC APPROACH

Development of a comprehensive yet flexible strategic approach allowed TTI to be responsive and proactive in its activity design and direction, rather than purely reactive to current events and trends. By developing and maintaining a good understanding of the social, political and economic context through the team's entire staff beyond just the Program Development Officers, key partners and data collection or analysis organizations, the project was able to gather critical information that allowed its programming to address the country's ever changing context. Additionally, the project's collaborative approach to activity design ensured grants were not designed in a vacuum with no regard for partner implementation preferences or approaches. This holistic strategy development process ensured that the final strategy was clear and not overly academic or complicated, allowing for greater adoption from grantees and the TTI team as well, further strengthening their understanding, resolve and shared sense of purpose. This was especially the case when describing who USAID was, what the U.S. government's goals were in coming to Tunisia, what the project's scope entailed (i.e. the project's definition of democracy and why it could not work on issues such as promotion of a secular government or religious advocacy) and, finally, why the project was ending, as without these key definitions the staff and grantees would not be able to fully disseminate the goals of respective activities.

The success of this methodology depended on the transparent selection of good partners and vendors, which helped to avoid unintended consequences with regards to perceptions of bias or preference; relying on a feedback loop of information from the entire team and their diverse

backgrounds, origins and perspectives to mitigate this and ensure a wide array of partners and geographies were successfully chosen rather than reliance on a select group of big name organizations based in the capital. TTI also recognized the importance of flexibility with regards to prioritization of certain geographical areas, as the degree of political disconnect shifted and certain areas became more or less influential due to the country's evolving political and security dynamics. For instance in the interior, while Sidi Bouzid was initially more symbolically important to the Revolution, Kef and Siliana became higher priorities due to the unrest and instability that emerged over the course of the program. Additionally, TTI was in effect the only program present in the interior, and its decision to emphasize this strategic area of the country yielded dividends in terms of positive change and adoption of TTI principles and goals.

This diverse network allowed TTI to be responsive to political changes in a variety of capacities, often involving innovative and flexible approaches to traditional transition issues as well as the use of technology and social media with the goal of taking activities' messages viral. By working with non-traditional community leaders and organizations, TTI was able to reach out to a wider array of audiences and subsequently gain insight into new potential avenues of programming, building greater partner capacity and professionalism. TTI worked with its partners to develop their ideas into clear and feasible action plans, providing guidance on the scheduling, resources, roles and scope to produce quality grants and procurements. This was particularly the case in times of uncertainty, such as the fall of 2013 when the political stagnation on the elections and the constitution created widespread frustration, but during which time TTI was still able to program effectively against its sub-objectives to encourage continued involvement and activism.

It was equally important to reinforce the role of Tunisian leaders in the development and ownership of the strategy. Garnering the buy-in of the entire team and developing quality localized sub-strategies while maintaining implementation for previously cleared grants took longer than anticipated and grant clearances were below target for two months immediately following the SRS. This could have been a missed opportunity to generate maximum impact against the newly developed sub-objectives. The team, and the strategy, proved the best response to this challenge; development staff in both offices committed to new, highly ambitious targets from August that have generated marked immediate impacts and allowed TTI to test the theory of change advanced in the strategy refinement.

In order to ensure quick responses, TTI found that through working closely with the Country Representative and Deputy Country Representative they could ensure activities were successfully implemented on shortened timetables rather than allowing multiple activity development revisions to delay implementation. Additionally, TTI struck a balance between activities which educated or raised awareness with those that provided tangible or visible proof of the Revolution's positive impact, depending on the goal of the activity, recognizing that oftentimes improved resources like equipped youth centers, renovated sports facilities, branded t-shirts and public art can achieve lasting effects and address disillusionment in diffuse audiences.

CLUSTERING AND LINKING ACTIVITIES

TTI employed a number of different clustering and linking methodologies in order to increase the effectiveness of its programming based on the eight initial sub-objectives designed under Phase Three: Activism, CVE, Marginalized Groups, Tolerance, Civic Engagement, CSO, Information, and (Social) Media. Grants were designed giving careful consideration of processes and procedures from concept design through to activity implementation for monitoring and evaluation purposes in order to better identify outputs, outcomes, and impact. This method was streamlined under the four consolidated sub-objectives (enhancing CSO leadership, fostering civic engagement and activism, enhancing participation of marginalized groups, and countering violent extremism), explicitly identifying for external and internal audiences the clear objectives that the program attempted to achieve.

These clusters created linkages between activities and partners, allowing for resiliency beyond the end of individual grants and the program writ large. Activities were explicitly designed to build and link upon each other, such partnering tangible DDGS activities like youth center equipment with soft impact engagement such as trainings, in order to create stronger impacts among target beneficiaries rather than disparate activities. Additionally, CSOs involved in TTI-organized debates, forums and trainings were able to join together for collective action and capacity growth while identifying and working towards joint solutions to problems of instability. TTI ensured standout participants or organizations working on activities in one cluster were identified and offered the ability to be involved in follow-on similar activities, such as youth participating in constitutional awareness training were also invited to join café politique discussions with other young people or present their experiences to inform resolution suggestions for local municipal leaders.

These overarching themes were further divided according to geographic distribution, with TTI identifying seven key governorates (Tunis, Ariana, Manouba, Ben Arous, Kasserine, Gafsa and Sidi Bouzid) as catalytic areas through which to focus their efforts due to the unique needs, capacities and sources of instability present in the interior versus the coastal communities. Geographic clusters built on the successes of past activities, sequencing events with established partners and target demographics in order to effectively expand and saturate given areas, thereby making progress towards stability objectives in more and more geographies. This also allowed the project to limit its national scope to a select number of large tolerance or democracy education activities, concentrating its efforts and activities otherwise to specific regions with specific issues rather than trying to cobble together several disparate regions and themes under one overly encompassing activity, thereby losing its efficacy and direction.

This strategy also helped to generate a sort of brand identity around important TTI themes with selected grantees, such as the multiple TEDx events held which engaged millions of Tunisians both in person and online by creating a community of like-minded individuals committed to new and innovative approaches to the transition on a variety of topics, ranging from women's rights to youth engagement, citizen activism and political transparency. Furthermore, by identifying key partners or types of activities for repeated engagement, TTI was able to strengthen and reinforce program priorities, such as conducting dance and art competitions at universities and youth centers, which were then targeted for information campaigns by volunteers identified in

A speaker presenting during the TEDx Spark event, focusing on the importance of women in Tunisian society

earlier activities and therefore became recognized in their communities as centers for positive change and havens for individuals looking to remain involved in the transition with like-minded citizens.

MONITORING AND EVALUATION

While TTI, led by its COP and Monitoring and Evaluation (M&E) Officer, incorporated an array of M&E components throughout its programming, it missed an opportunity to more definitively gauge its impact over time by not conducting a comprehensive baseline survey upon initial program implementation. While several activities were conducted over the course of the program on select areas such as CVE and political awareness, an initial survey would have served to better inform strategy, activity development and partner identification at the outset, establishing a stronger platform for future programming.

TTI also emphasized the importance of developing M&E plans in a participatory way with the entire team during the activity development stage, with plans including realistic indicators and targets which are measurable and practical. Furthermore, due to the inability for the M&E officer or respective PDO to attend each and every event, TTI relied on its Grant Managers, Procurement and Logistics Officers and Drivers to collect critical qualitative data on its activities' impacts and challenges, thereby requiring the entire team to be literate in the type of information needed and what each activity was designed to achieve in order for there to be shared understanding and commitment to its success. To attain this, it was important to develop and follow M&E procedures that were efficient and consistently followed in all offices, with senior management providing emphasis and oversight. Beyond the team, grantees also needed to be informed of the importance of M&E and its role throughout the entire activity cycle; grantees needed to be held accountable for providing both quantitative and qualitative data.

Finally, given the project's diverse programming areas and approaches, holding lessons learned sessions after the conclusion of every activity again with the entire team would help strengthen the project's impact and foster an environment which was collaborative and responsive for team members in all areas. Sharing outcomes and outputs within the team, including failures or problems, would help the team to learn from its mistakes and anticipate implementation challenges in the future and over the long term.

IN-KIND AND FOG MECHANISMS

TTI aimed to promote civic engagement through small community development projects connecting local economic development to national decision-making by working in marginalized communities to enable them to participate in the political process. To that end, In Kind grants under contract were the preferred mechanism to deliver goods and services, with the financial and management system requirements for awardees proportional to the complexity and cost value of the grant. When designing activities, TTI considered which suggested activities would achieve the impacts that, when taken together, would advance the sub-objectives and benefit the appropriate beneficiaries most successfully, and therefore which mechanism would enable both the success of the activity and the capacity building of the awardee. As such, TTI developed a graduated approach to the selection of small local organizations for FOGs, in certain circumstances beginning with In Kind assistance and maturing to FOG mechanisms when appropriate if and when capacity was established.

Selection of the appropriate grant award mechanism was particularly important given that following the Revolution and the opening of the civil society space, Tunisia experienced an explosion of newly created CSOs, often with great enthusiasm but less than desirous capacity, and sometimes working at cross purposes due to oversaturation in one area and noticeable lack of involvement in other critical spaces. Many of these organizations required leadership training, while others could benefit from working in closer collaboration with their regional networks in order to achieve a more effective level of impact and more cohesive field of implementation. As such, TTI was required to not only be very selective in terms of the awardees chosen for FOG implementation versus In Kind, but also ensure that its target objectives were met through selection of the right mechanism to deliver immediate results. For short-term, low cost GUCs, grantees were required primarily to demonstrate their technical ability to implement the activity; longer-term and higher value grants required the technical knowledge as well as demonstrated abilities to manage the in-kind resources or FOG milestones.

All organizations interested in partnering with TTI needed to demonstrate technical experience or capacity in the field of the proposed activity, showing evidence of institutional capacity or willingness to participate in capacity building activities. In terms of the activity itself, awardees were required to justify the reasonableness of the size, type and cost of the proposed activities, as well as the effectiveness of the proposed means for implementing the grant. Discussions were then held with the assigned Grant Manager or Procurement and Logistics Officer about how the activity met with the program's goals and their organizational capacities, developing a work plan describing each step of the activity and the method through which monitoring and evaluation would be achieved. Additionally, the budget would receive scrupulous review to detail all costs required for the activity and the best method through which those costs could be recouped, be it through In Kind or FOG implementation. Furthermore, for certain types of activities, such as neighborhood cleanup and rehabilitation and youth center and sporting activities in particular, In Kind methods proved to be the ideal approach for delivering optimal good and services in a timely fashion for organizations lacking the financial, logistical or managerial ability to do so on their own. Field work and thorough M&E from past activities was deemed essential in order to identify and design projects from an informed position with regards to both outcome achievement and implementation method.

QUICK RESPONSE FRAMEWORK

Through the implementation of the project's Quick Response Framework (QRF) activities, providing material and technical support to communities, CSOs and local institutions, TTI helped to build democratic resilience, increase citizen participation in democratic life, and bolster positive change. To achieve these objectives, the program worked with a variety of Tunisian individuals, organizations and government bodies to identify and implement key programmatic initiatives that were catalytic in nature, with activities primarily focused on two key areas: encouraging new and emerging civil society groups to contribute to the national dialogue and promoting civic engagement through small community development projects. Utilizing the QRF and in accordance with OTI's programming approach, TTI's activity strategy was designed to be flexible and responsive to changing conditions and needs as the political environment evolved, laying the foundation for sustainable solutions. Activity sectors addressed an array of themes, including civic engagement, transparent and responsive governance, communication, tolerance and pluralism, leadership and countering violent extremism.

TTI found that in order to reach the desired impact in one area through this methodology, it was most advantageous to do more than one activity in carefully selected or targeted areas, building on previous activities to develop new actions and establish a recognizable narrative of peace and positive engagement. The project further coordinated carefully with other donors so as to not duplicate efforts, nor leave key elements of society excluded. Beyond international donors, TTI noted the importance of working with respected local associations with access to decision makers in order to influence long lasting change and facilitate community action. Oftentimes, this community support was delivered in the form of youth centers whose ties to at risk students, their parents and municipal leaders proved essential to identifying winning activity designs and reinforcing their message to increase impact. In addition to holding events at youth centers, the project also found success organizing big events involving famous artists or performers on symbolic dates to advocate for the unity of Tunisians, capitalizing on the inherent patriotism and shared values or popularity they could afford.

Finally, TTI designed Quick Response activities in terms of coherent campaigns, not just results frameworks, looking outward rather than behind for activity ideas. Campaigns such as "We Are Different, But Do Not Have Differences," "We Are Different, But We Must Stay United," "Be A

Piece Of The Solution," and "I Love Siliana" were all examples of activities which created buzz and strong brand identity beyond just awareness or excitement in order to catalyze action. They also utilized a multi-tiered approach to message dissemination, incorporating internet spots, TV and radio broadcasts, billboard production, social media sites, viral video and DDGS procurement of goods with campaign slogans or logos distributed by informed volunteers or awardees in carefully selected venues in order to increase both the breadth and depth of exposure and recognition, informing, educating and engaging Tunisians on multiple levels to reach the desired impact and empowering individuals to promote tolerance and combat violence in their communities.

COUNTERING VIOLENT EXTREMISM

In spring of 2013 OTI/W undertook a desk study which served as a key source of baseline data upon which to develop the program's pilot CVE component. This study defined the nature of the Salafist threat in Tunisia, noting the dramatic and sudden increase in Islamic organizations, the three largest of which formed Le Front Tunisien des Associations Islamiques which became a key lobbying force in the pro-Sharia law movement. Salafists after the fall of the Ben Ali regime battled to control the country's network of mosques as a pulpit from which to spread their message of intolerance and violence, exerting the influence through a combination of coercion, intimidation and the provision of benefits and services. Their recruitment tactics included "preaching tours," strong social media presence on such sites as Facebook, the use of charities as fronts for Salafist recruitment, and targeting of young men in particular through activities which incorporated the arts, music, sport and other leisure activities.

Driving violent extremism in Tunisia were a variety of factors, including the declining economic condition, regional disparities, increased operating space as a result of the newfound political freedom, weakness on the part of security forces (particularly along the border with Libya), Ennahda's refusal to take a hard line against the Salafists for fear of alienating its conservative constituents, and finally a disillusionment and disengagement in the post revolutionary political arena on the part of youth. To address these various drivers, TTI's CVE programming addressed issues of identity and fostered a sense of belonging to moderate Tunisian society for at risk youth by using sporting events, use of new media, incorporation of the arts, creation of socially inclusive activities and prioritization of strategically identified cities and neighborhoods where the pull of extremism were most strongly felt for its programming implementation.

A group of youth take part in "Beatmaking in the Interior," designed to engage youth through music and the arts against violent extremism

This approach allowed TTI to generate impact in several discrete areas. Activities such as the refurbishment of youth centers, creation of dance or performance groups, support to sports teams, development of artistic skills and education about alternate means of non-violent expression gave youth the ability to discuss sensitive topics through positive means while also recognizing these avenues as viable alternatives that many of their peers likewise supported and wanted to engage in. This increased participation in moderate youth organizations furthermore organically created opportunities for youth leaders to emerge and develop their skills, expanding the impact of the activities and creating resiliency beyond the relatively short implementation period. By targeting the enabling environment in select areas versus a more diffuse approach of focusing on at risk populations writ large, programming better established community buy in and ownership. The inherent short term activity periods and their intensive nature were significant challenges, but the project overcame them by building the capacity and respect for local community leaders such as youth center directors who could outlast the length of the activities and serve as positive counterpoints to the sustained engagement and constant presence of extremist influences. This was especially true as the short time frame of activities and small grants nature of the program precluded it from establishing comprehensive and formal alternative structures.

Given the lack of comprehensive data on violent extremism recruiting data at the outset of the program the OTI programming team used situational knowledge and analysis of the contemporary environment to identify two locations where CVE programming could have the largest impact, one in Greater Tunis and one in Kasserine. Both areas selected were breeding grounds for extremists with large youth populations and underserved government services. In order to confirm not only the geographic selection but also the strategic approach, TTI secured the services of a research and analysis firm to conduct two comprehensive surveys of each area, the first in September of 2013 to establish a baseline and the second in March of 2014 to capture changes and impact. Both studies provided critical information about the operating environment and programming impacts to inform future activities, as well as confirmation of the strategic approach.

WORKING WITH LOCAL PARTNERS: CSOS AND GOVERNMENT

Early and often community engagement on a local level (i.e., involvement in the design of activities, consultation with the community) led to significant ownership, motivation, presumed longer-term impact of TTI's activities, acknowledging the importance of improved municipal relationships with citizens and the fact that national staff often were too constrained to provide longer term engagement. The participatory process leant more transparency from the perspective of the communities targeted and helped to build trust between the country's different stakeholders quickly, strengthening the sense of ownership among CSOs members in particular. TTI achieved greater cooperation and success in its interactions with various CSOs by placing great importance on understanding respective organizations' needs and ideas, while balancing that with clear communication on the program's objectives, capabilities and methodologies.

In order to improve this cooperation, TTI identified and mentored standout CSOs to achieve a higher level of proficiency and autonomy through their "learning by doing approach," thus ensuring greater success for its activities and providing additional opportunities for NGOs to strengthen themselves and connect with larger networks within their communities and beyond. Working with nascent CSOs in particular, TTI recognized that their enthusiasm and dedication were key traits that could not be taught, but that in order to achieve success they had to be combined with professionalism, organized program management and resource development. Activities often included communication consultation, budgeting advice, guidance on how to network and leverage existing resources, and direction in terms of scope and impact that built their capacity and set them on the path to resiliency.

These organizations in turn contributed with new ways to more successfully disseminate information to the public, new activity ideas to reach target demographics, and qualitative data to better inform future programming. In order to ensure longer lasting support for these organizations and their endeavors, TTI reinforced the importance of cooperation with political partners and authorities in order to encourage positive interaction between the government and its citizens, even in the face of administrative and political constraints.

A group of youth attending the opening of a new park in their neighborhood which was constructed with support from local officials

As such, TTI was able to connect these capable CSOs with equally progressive and engaging municipal government leaders, demonstrating to both the opportunities for positive partnership and engagement on areas of mutual interest. In order to facilitate these connections and demonstrate for both parties the efficacy of the project's activities and objectives, TTI ensured that Tunisian government officials were invited to attend CSO-led activities, being de facto sponsors, guest speakers and partners in various activities. Intensive consultation in general took place between CSOs and government officials to prepare agendas for joint forums (on the issues, presenters, presentations, break-out sessions on specific topics), debates, and resolutions or manifestos generated to ensure better collaboration and thus success in resolving the country's socio-economic and political issues. That being said, the project took special care to ensure that activities did not favor one party or platform outright, remaining non-partisan and engaging mostly with municipal leaders whose ties to their respective communities could supersede partisan politics. TTI also found that the presence of local and central government officials helped ensure greater media coverage and community turnout, encouraging local and national media outlets to cover events and increase the activities' visibility during critical periods where multiple initiatives were taking place across the country with various partners and priorities.

OPERATIONAL COMPONENTS

In order to achieve programmatic success, TTI relied on its operational structures to provide the support and resources needed for a one team approach. This started with hiring the right local staff to identify the most suitable employees; multiple reference checks and use of a local recruitment company that understands the local market around each office would ensure selectivity in terms of quality but also diversity in terms of backgrounds and experience. Onboarding new team members can be challenging and may cause a delay in implementation due to the need to train and bring up to speed less experienced staff, improving staff retention was achieved especially in Phase Three through provision of comprehensive training so staff can successfully carry out their specific functions; development of clear scopes of work to avoid unnecessary duplication of effort as well as understanding about the critical roles everyone play in supporting the team as a whole; and production of well defined and easy to adopt manuals that everyone can access; and involving national staff in decision making and strategy definition through the creation of the Senior Strategy Team. DAI funded a February 2013 STTA to customize, adapt and train the entire staff on a refreshed Field Operations Manual that would become the authoritative reference on local procedures. By including national staff on the Senior Strategy team and prioritizing the creation of leaders within the staff, TTI emphasized the importance and value it placed on the success of its team, not just the success of its activities.

To ensure this success, TTI invested in team building and placed a high importance on bringing the Tunis and Sbeitla regional office staff together, both within the context of SRSs and without in order to develop a strong team spirit and allow for organic exchange of information and support. TTI also considered holding meetings between people with the same position but different offices, not to mention exchanges so as to better understand the context of their respective counterparts and seek out efficiencies. Senior leadership in Tunis also recognized the importance of spending time in the regional offices to ensure staff there received the attention and opportunities needed to succeed. The COP and Operations Manager instilled a sense of discipline and professionalism in the staff, so that team members took ownership and pride in their work and differentiated between personal and professional relationships.

ANNEX A: MAP OF TTI GOVERNORATES

OTI ACTIVITIES IN TUNISIA
AT PROGRAM CLOSE-OUT

TUNISIA WIDE

ACTIVITY SECTORS

- Civic Engagement
- Communication
- Countering Violent Extremism
- Leadership
- Tolerance & Pluralism
- Transparent & Responsive Governance

**Program Total:
272 Activities**

Map Created 6.27.2014

The boundaries and names used on this map do not imply official endorsement or acceptance by the U.S. Government.

TUNISIA

Bizerte

BIZERTE   ARIANA   **TUNIS**

MANOUBA Ariana   NABEUL

Manouba   Ben Arous

Beja   BEJA   BEN AROUS

BEJA

JENDOUBA   Zaghouan   Nabeul

Jendouba   SILIANA   ZAGHOUAN

SOUSSE

El Tarf   **TOTAL**

Kef   Siliana   272 Activities
for $9,878,767

KEF   Siliana   Kairouan   Sousse

KAIROUAN   Monastir
MONASTIR

ALGERIA   Thala   MAHDIA

KASSERINE   Sbeitla   El Djem   Mahdia

Kasserine   Sidi
Bouzid

SIDI BOUZID   SFAX

Sfax

GAFSA   Mahares

Gafsa

Skhira

TOZEUR   Tozeur   Houmt
Souk

Nefta   El Hamma   Gabes   Zarzis

GABES

Kebili   Matmata   MEDENINE

KEBILI   Medenine   Ben Guerdane

Tataouine

TATAOUINE   Dehibat   LIBYA

ACTIVITY FUNDING

- Up to $10,000
- $10,001 - $25,000
- $25,001 - $100,000
- $100,001 - $250,000
- $250,001 - $650,000

Note: One dot may represent
multiple activities.

Date of Data: 6.23.2014
Date of Map Creation: 6.25.2014

The boundaries and names used on this
map do not imply official endorsement or
acceptance by the U.S. Government.

0 10 20 30 40
mi
0   30   60   90   km

**FUNDING FOR
REGIONAL ACTIVITIES**

Up to $10,000
$10,001 - $25,000
$25,001 - $50,000
$50,001 - $100,000
$100,001 - $500,000

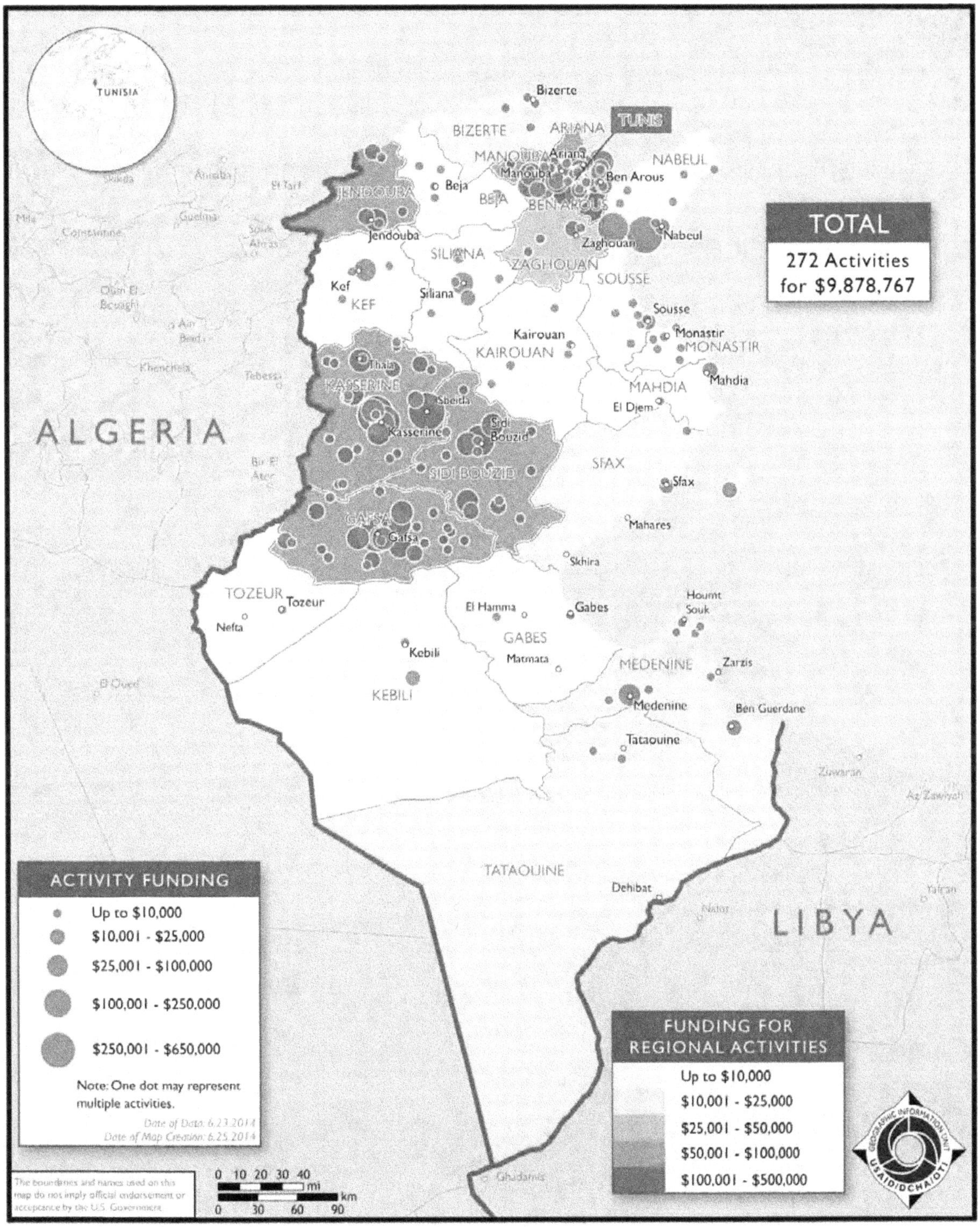

ANNEX B: PROGRAMMING HIGHLIGHTS AND CHARTS

ACTIVITIES SUMMARY

Since program inception in May of 2011, DAI funded 272 activities valued at $12,421,042 and partnered with over 180 different organizational groups, government entities, consultants and vendors. The below graphs demonstrate the activity distributions according to a variety of data sets, including by office, sector, organizational type, region, agreement, grant type, and over time.

ACTIVITIES BY OFFICE AND REGION

Through its two field offices, TTI was able to program in all 24 governorates of Tunisia. The below charts break down the 115 activities sponsored by the Sbeitla Office and the 157 activities sponsored by the Tunis Office according to geography.

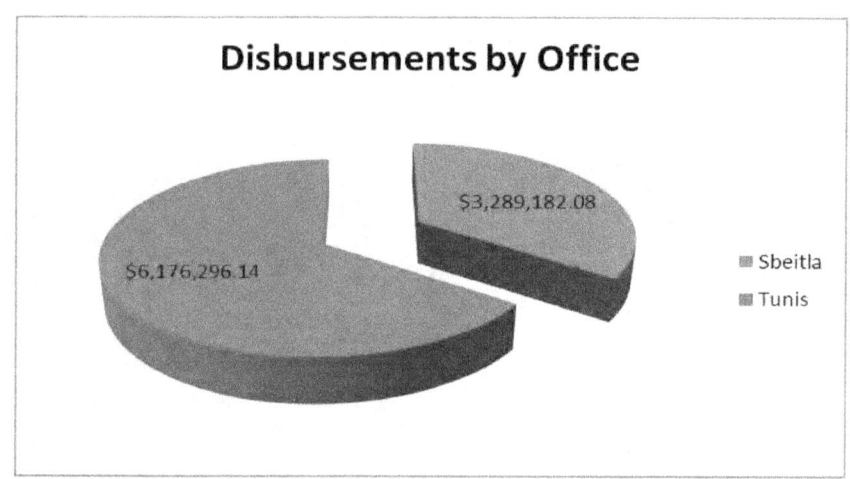

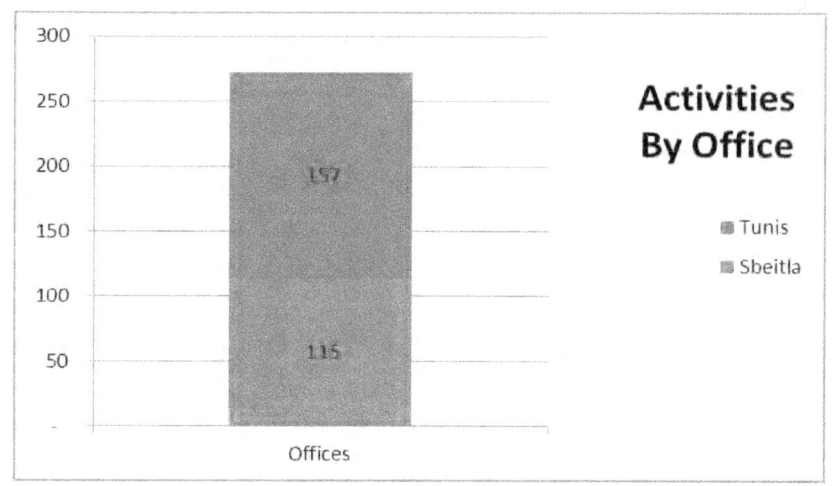

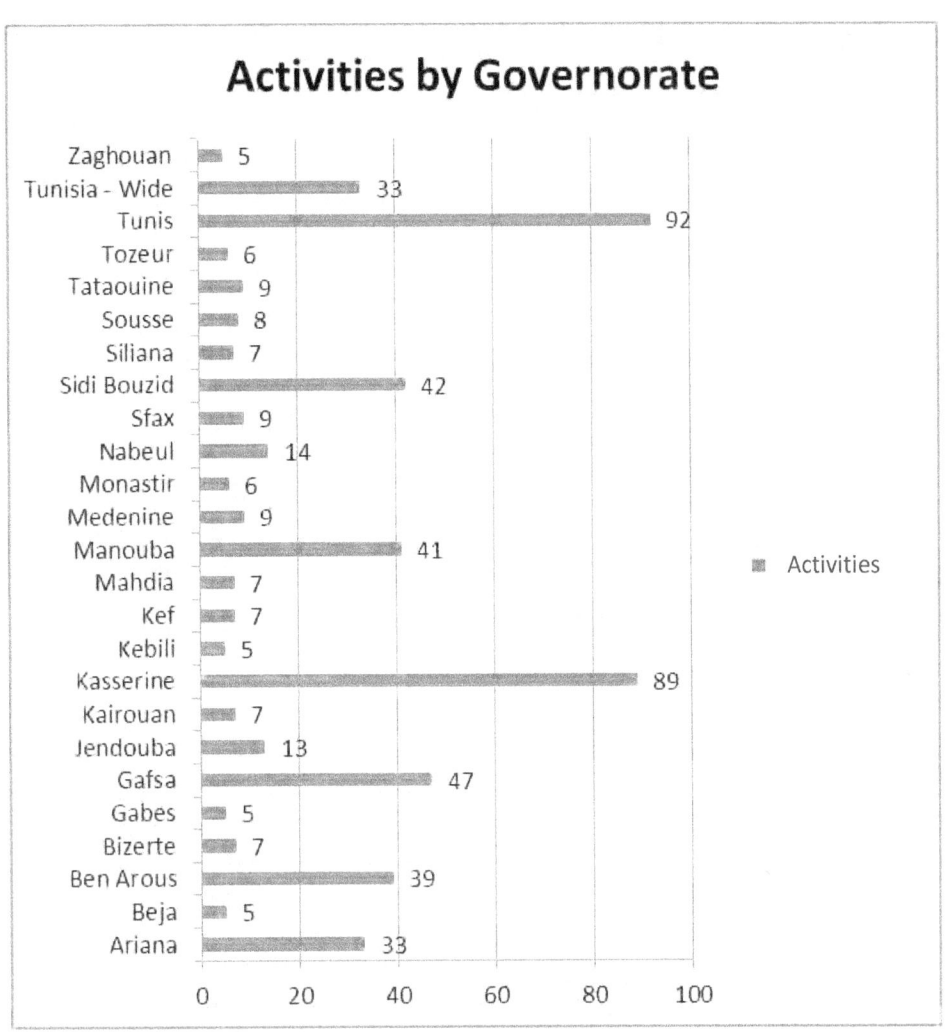

Activities by Governorate

Governorate	Activities
Zaghouan	5
Tunisia - Wide	33
Tunis	92
Tozeur	6
Tataouine	9
Sousse	8
Siliana	7
Sidi Bouzid	42
Sfax	9
Nabeul	14
Monastir	6
Medenine	9
Manouba	41
Mahdia	7
Kef	7
Kebili	5
Kasserine	89
Kairouan	7
Jendouba	13
Gafsa	47
Gabes	5
Bizerte	7
Ben Arous	39
Beja	5
Ariana	33

ACTIVITIES BY SECTOR

TTI undertook activities according to nine specific sectors which correlated to its devised sub-objectives to achieve peace and security: Civic Education, Civic Engagement, Civil Society, Communication, CVE, Leadership, Tolerance and Pluralism, Transparent and Responsive Governance, and Youth Empowerment. The below charts outline the activities by sector according to the amounts disbursed and the number of activities undertaken in each.

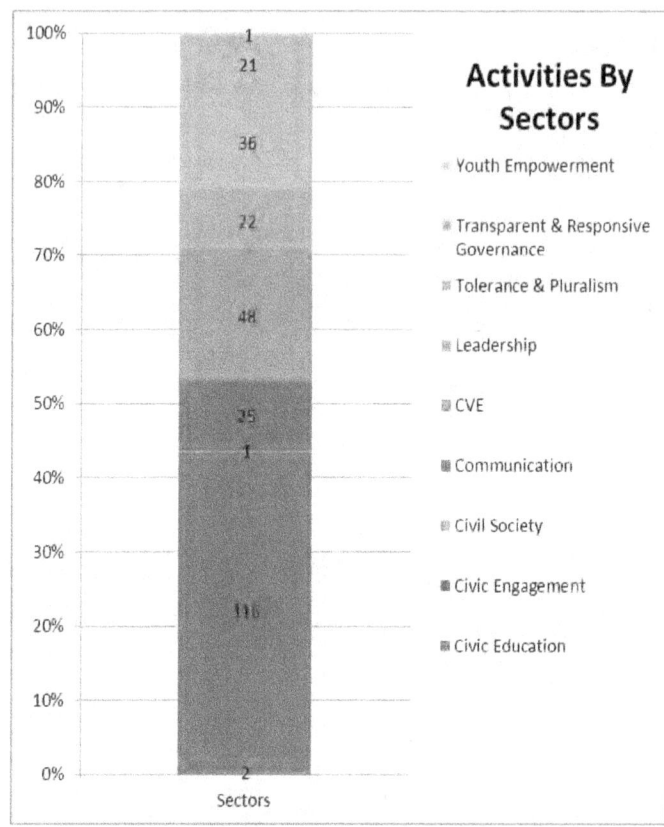

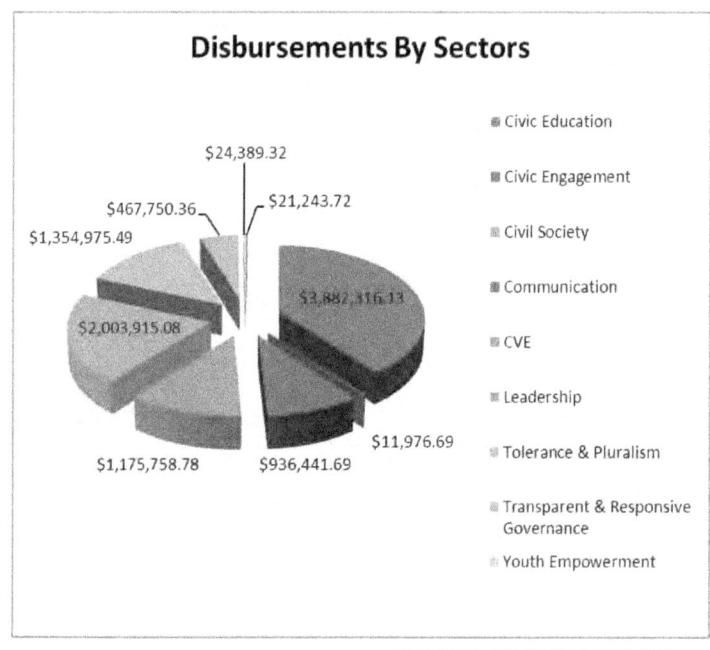

ACTIVITIES BY GRANT TYPE

As a small grants program, TTI typically employed grant under contract (GUC) mechanisms in order to partner with its awardees. Approximately 87% of its activities utilized the GUC mechanism, while 10% were direct distribution of goods and services (DDGS) and 3% were allocated towards short term technical assistance (STTA). Within these three methods, TTI executed the activities through six different agreement formats: Fixed Obligation Grants (FOG), In Kind Grants (IK), Limited Scope Grant Agreements (LSGA), Standard Grants (SG), Purchase Orders (PO), and STTA Employment Agreements.

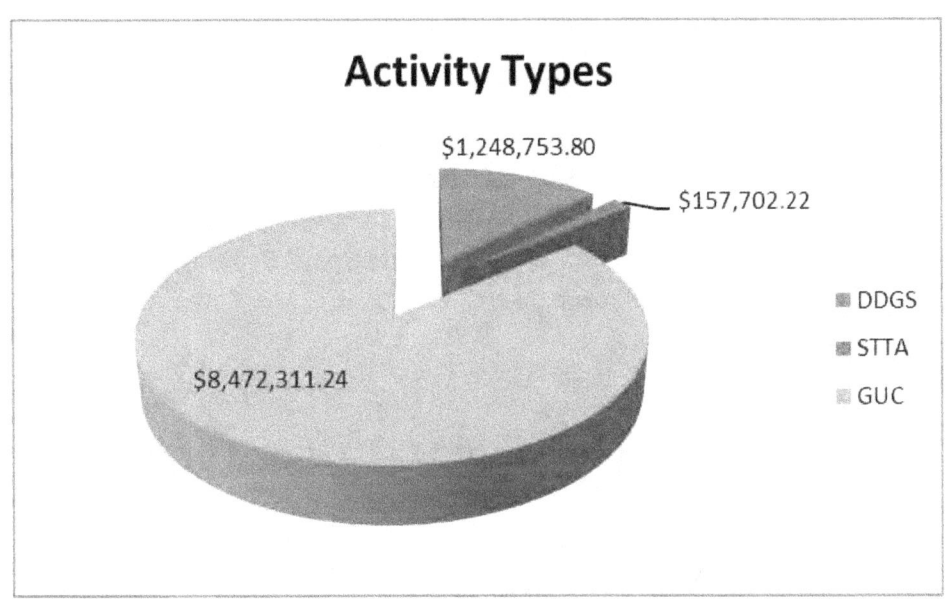

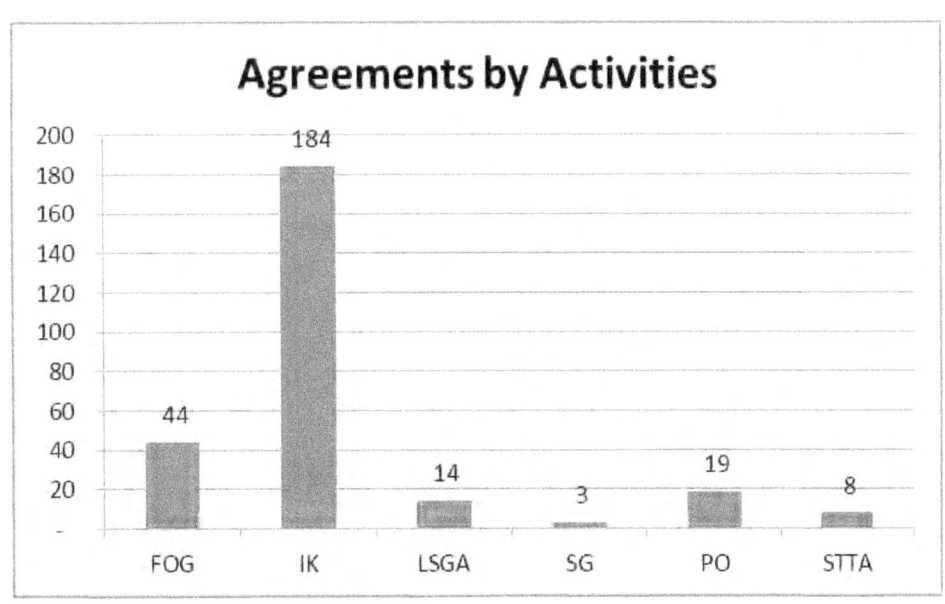

ACTIVITIES DISBURSED OVER TIME

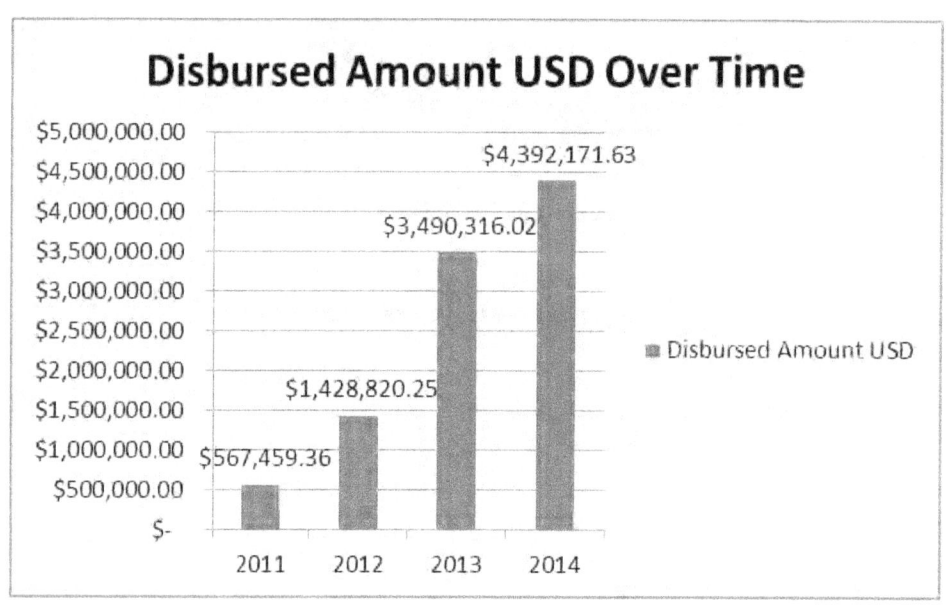

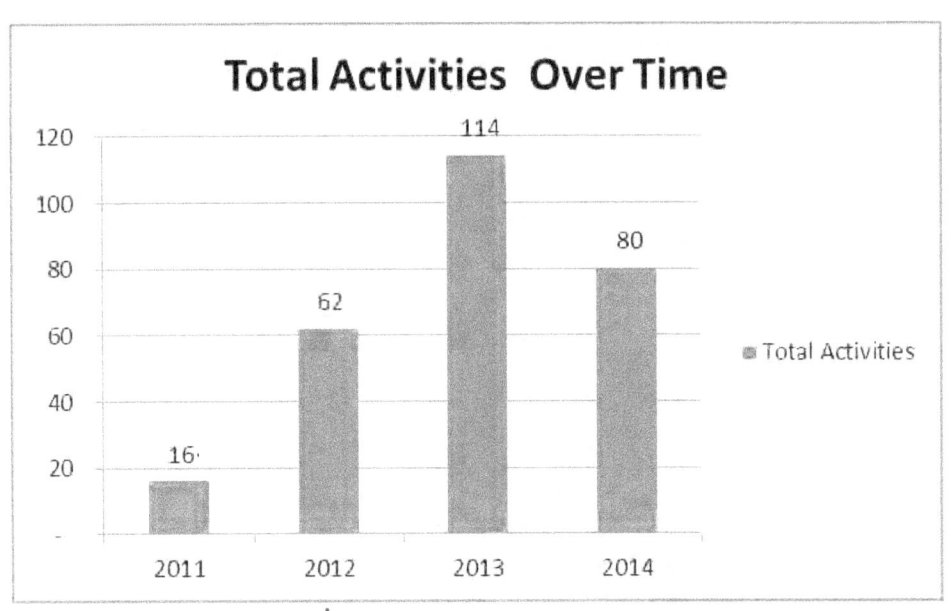

ACTIVITIES BY ORGANIZATION TYPE

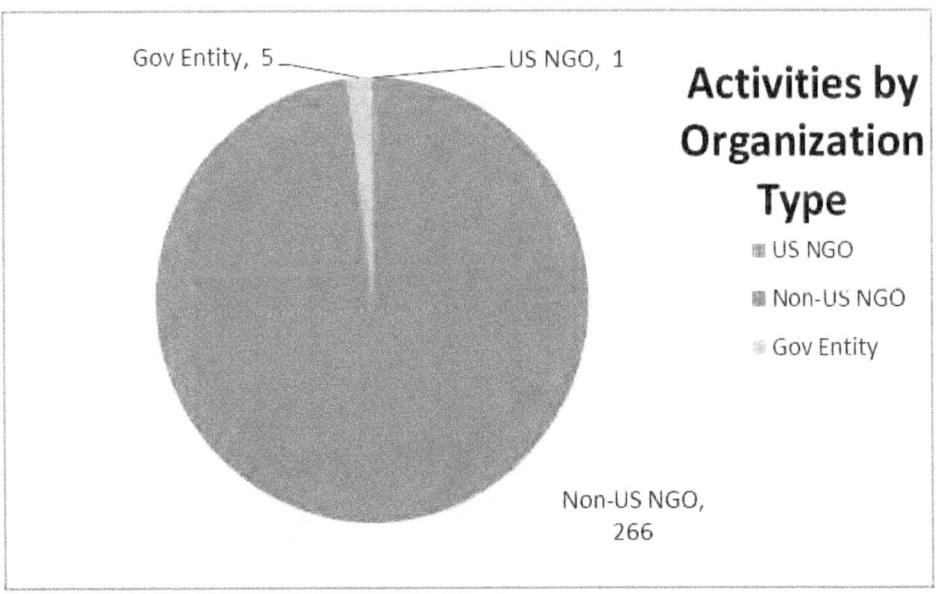

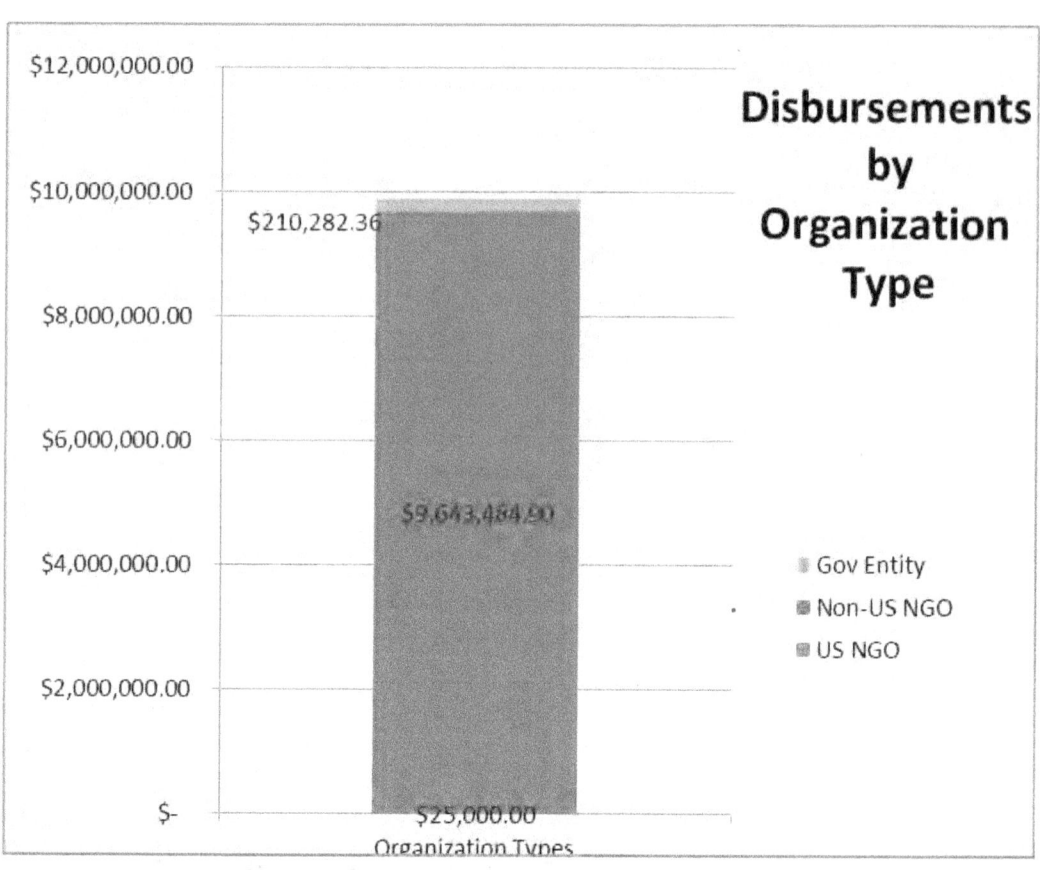

www.ingramcontent.com/pod-product-compliance
Lightning Source LLC
Chambersburg PA
CBHW080518290526
45790CB00006B/2217

9 781508 601395